Kuṇḍalinī

Stilled or Stirred?

Kuṇḍalinī

Stilled or Stirred?

Swami Veda Bharati

Cataloging in Publication Data — DK
[Courtesy: D.K. Agencies (P) Ltd. <docinfo@dkagencies.com>]

Vedabhāratī, *Svāmī,* 1933-
Kuṇḍalinī : stilled or stirred? / Swami Veda Bharati.
p. cm.
Includes bibliographical references.
ISBN 9788124606667

1. Kuṇḍalinī. I. Title.

DDC 294.5436 23

ISBN 13 : 978-81-246-0666-7 (HB)
ISBN 13 : 978-81-246-0667-4 (PB)
First published in India in 2013

Printed and published by:
D.K. Printworld (P) Ltd.
Regd. Office : 'Vedasri', F-395, Sudarshan Park
(Metro Station: Ramesh Nagar)
New Delhi – 110 015
Phones : (011) 2545 3975, 2546 6019; *Fax* : 2546 5926
e-mail : indology@dkprintworld.com
Web : www.dkprintworld.com

in association with

AHYMSIN Publishers
Swami Rama Sadhaka Grama (SRSG)
Virpur Khurd, Virbhadra Road
Rishikesh (UA). India Pin: 249 203
Phones: (0135) 245 3030; *Fax*: 243 1582
e-mail:<ahymsinpublishers@gmail.com>/<info@ahymsin.in>
Website: www.ahymsin.in

Surrender

To His Sun-fire I surrender this love offering so its meaning may become a new dawn in the mind horizons of the reader.

His uncoiled lightning struck out touching a tongue of his flame to my fontanella, the softest spot in a newborn, that I was to Him.

All the lotuses lit up blooming in the lakes of my Sarasvatī the river of mystical knowing. Then I knew I am the coiled-up serpent of consciousness as I await further uncoilings. Again by the touch of His Grace.

Description of cover and inside photos

Cover: In the ancient traditions of the Mayas of Guatemala many sculptures and carvings are seen with lilies sprouting from body locations that can be easily identified with the *yoga* concept of *cakra*s which are depicted as lotuses. The picture on the front cover is one such carving from the museum at the Tikal pyramids.

The picture on the inside title page of a statuette of a person in meditation was taken from an image seen in a small private collection on a tiny island in the middle of Lake Peten Itza in the vicinity of the town of Flores (gateway to the Tikal pyramids). The source location of the statuette could not be determined upon asking the owner who had many other similar statuettes.

Foreword

THIS presentation first started with attempts to answer some questions from our meditation initiates. Then a number of transcripts of lectures given at various locations were added, amended and edited. It is hoped that the readers will find the common theme of *kuṇḍalinī* through all the chapters of this collection helpful in their spiritual quests.

The thoughts presented are a result of the experiences granted by the grace of my *gurudeva*, Swami Rama of the Himalayas, and his lineage. Nothing here is imaginary but a reality of inner spaces.

We are confluences of rivers of forces that criss-cross this universe, time, space and consciousness. When we learn to take a sacred dip into this confluence, that is our true identity, we realize that all that was feeble was a fearsome illusion and here now we regain our one and only self.

The conscious and unconscious forces that traverse this universe are the building materials of both the universe and our very being. In this, the boundaries between us and the universe are imagined ones, like segmenting a river, giving different names to the segments and engineering conflict among thus named segments of the same river. It is like drawing with a chalk boundaries between my ocean and yours. The waves of forces wipe out the chalk marks in less than an instant. This wiping out of the marks is called love as well as aesthetic appreciation of universal beauty.

A master of *kuṇḍalinī* is a master beautician and an artistic appreciator of the painting called the universe. This painting is on the canvas of the mind. The painting is the mind. The colours are of the mind. Easel and the brush are of the mind. The wall on which the painting hangs is also the mind. So says the unique lyrical philosophical text titled *Yoga-Vāsiṣṭha*. The one who appreciates the painting is a figure painted as part of the painting. Such is the paradox of our divisions of "I" and "thou".

The confluent *kuṇḍalinī* which we present in this treatise is the only force of which all the other forces are tributaries. It is the river of unity. When one has taken a dip in this sacred confluence, all s/he can see is beauty and love, and exclaims: Oh, what a beautiful loving world!

The all-creation, too, sings with her/him: Oh, what a beautiful loving world!

S/he then proceeds to ensure that nothing happens to stain or mar such a beauty. S/he then proceeds to draw all light-sparks, called souls, to walk the path to this confluence where union is the prime song and separation of dualities is an interesting myth.

May your reading this presentation help you appreciate the beauty of this myth also and then guide you to transcend the same into eternal union. "Many" and the "other" are then abolished. There is no more confluence of many. There is not even one, for one is a number. There is only infinity.

May you be Mono and Solo[1] in such infinity in this very life and no "other" exist thereafter.

---

[1] From *dios*, god or God, *deva*. *Diosa*, our translation of *devī*, feminine form of *deva*.

Acknowledgements

I WOULD like to thank all those who have helped in making this publication a success. Among the many I would like to specifically mention are Lalita Arya, Dowlat Budhram, Bhola Shankar Dabral, John C. Gage and Stomya Persaud.

Special thanks are due to Sri Vamadeva Sastri (David Frawley) for his quote on the *suṣumṇā*. Thanks also to Angiras Arya for his help in designing the front cover for the digital copy.

I also thank Juan Burwell for designing the cover of this book.

Swami Veda Bharati

Contents

Introduction
Tantra: Clearing Misunderstandings

WRITING on Tantra is like trying to count the atoms in the universe or weigh the salt in the oceans.

Tantra is an exposition of *śrī-vidyā,* i.e. the metascience that provides the rules by which all sciences operate and whereby the universe is governed.

The substance of Tantra is the Vedic *tantu,* the thread that is stretched throughout the universe — *tantum tatam.*

> *tiraśchino vi-tato raśmir eṣām adhaḥ svid asid upari svid āsīt* |
>
> This thread is the ray that folds and unfolds as it is stretched across the universe, below and above.
>
> — *Ṛgveda*

> *yo vidyat sūtram vi-tatam yasminn otaḥ prajā imaḥ* |
>
> It is the thread, the *sūtra,* onto which all beings and entities are strung. — *Atharvaveda*

As this ray of the light of consciousness folds upon itself, it is seen as a coil, a *kuṇḍala,* forming the coiled energies of the conscious universe, becoming *kuṇḍalinī.* It may also be called *tantra,* the fabric woven of the thread, the grid of the universe. The primary meaning of the word *tantra* is a grid of energies by the tāntric formula:

sarvaṁ śaktimayam jagat |

The entire universe is comprised of energies and potencies.

The *śakti*s which are all diversifications of one *śakti*, the *mahā-śakti.*

yasyonmeṣa-nimeṣābhyam jagataḥ pralayodayau |
tam śakti-cakra-vibhāva-prabhavam śaṅkaram namaḥ ||

By whose outwinking and inwinking the manifestation and dissolution of the universe proceed,

We laud Him who is the generator of peace — *śaṁ-kara,* the Source and the ruling Lord of the varieties of the wheels of *śakti*s.

śaktayo 'sya jagat sarvam |

The entire universe is His *śakti*s.

Thus all personalities, entities and objects, macrocosmic or microcosmic, are nothing but a continuum of waves — *spanda* of the One Awesome Tremendous One — *bhairava.*

jalasyevormayo vahner jvālā-bhaṅgyaḥ prabhā raveḥ |
mamaiva bhairavasyaita viśva-bhaṅgyo ni-veditaḥ ||

Like the waves of water,
Like the flames of fire,
Like the light(s) of the sun
All these forms and entities are *śakti*s of Me,
The Awesome One, presented.

A person initiated into this awareness does not view any parts of this consciousness piecemeal. For such a one, the entire universe is but one *śakti.*

ananta-koṭi-brahmāṇḍa-brahma-vyāpaka-rūpiṇīm |

> Whose form is nothing but pervasion through all creative beings — *brahmas* of countless myriad universes.

Here we need to break all our habits of thoughts. The concepts of "I versus another", "body other than the soul", "the earth below against the sun above", male–female dichotomies, and whatever else separates any cognition-unit from another cognition-unit must be relinquished. All our values about phenomena must be jettisoned. We read in the *Yoga-Vāsiṣṭha*:

> *na bahir nāntare nādho nordhvam arthe na śūnyake* |
>
> Not outside, nor inside, not below, nor above, neither in reality nor yet in the Null.

Here we give an example of how our concepts of space and time are absolutely without any validity. Before embarking on a voyage, a religiously-minded astronaut prays, "Lord in Heaven above, protect me on this journey". As he lifts his eyes up he sees the moon in the sky. Later he lands on the moon. He now wishes to thank God for the safe journey. He lifts his eyes up to the heavens, and what does he see above? He sees the earth, up in the sky above. Shall he say, "I thank the Lord Who is on the Earth"?

Every notion or every mental association, however seemingly natural, of ours has to be renounced in order to qualify for initiation into the Tantra path.

Thus to say that "there is a *kuṇḍalinī* within us" is erroneous. There is no distinction between *within* and *without*. It is the *devātma-śakti* (the power of the divine self) that is *kuṇḍalinī*. That self is all-pervading. A beginning level student often asks: Are the *cakra*s in the spine or in the front?

So long as one asks such a question s/he is not yet initiated. In a magnetic field, is the field in front of the magnet or in the back? A tāntric initiate drops these notions of "*kuṇḍalinī* inside us", of a "*cakra* in the heart centre in front", of a "*kuṇḍalinī* in the back, in the spine". There are no such locations.

Initially we fail to abandon these thought-habits, these artificial imprints, so that one looks for *mūlādhāra cakra* at the base of the spine. The *kuṇḍalinī*'s *diosa*-morphic[1] representation is the goddess of all gods and goddesses, Pārvatī.

> Pārvatī yearns for a union with Her eternal Lord and undertakes the most difficult of ascesis (*tapasyā*). She goes on a fast. First she lives on fruits. She abandons those and lives on a diet of leaves, petals. Then the leaves and petals also disappear and only a slim vine-like Pārvatī remains. She is then called *a-parṇa* (the petal-less one). It is after such a penance that her Lord appears before her.

We see in the parable that when Pārvatī has left the fruits of *karma* behind, fasted only on leaves and petals of *cakra*s and has finally dropped them, She becomes *a-parṇa* (without petals). Then the vine of *kuṇḍalinī* is leafless, and what was conceived as a line now contracts only to a dot (a *bindu*) which has no magnitude.

Our present way of thinking about these "internal" events undergoes total alteration as our realizations grow. The way the processes of Euclid are correct for a student in the sixth class at school but inapplicable, invalid, in quantum physics, so also whatever is valid in our daily transactions becomes invalid to the tāntric initiate.

---

[1] Our neologism, *diosa*-femine of Spanish *Dios* for God. There is no English equivalent for "Goddess", although there are many "goddesses".

Much of our thinking about Tantra these days is guesswork, speculation, and not based on direct knowledge. Until such direct knowledge ensues, all the philosophical discussions and acts of worship are valid and often helpful. But for the true initiate:

pūjā nāma na puṣpadyair ya matiḥ kriyate dr̥ḍha ।
nirvikalpe pare vyomni sa pūjā hy adaral layaḥ ॥

> That is no *pūjā* (worship ritual) where with flowers and flame the externalized view of life is further strengthened; the true *pūjā* is the dissolution of oneself into the trans-distinctive Supreme Space.

These are just a few of the statements in all the sixty-four Tantras that depict the ultimate in Tantra. All else are steps to be taken by toddlers like ourselves.

Having stated the transcendental goal of Tantra, we come to a few commonly raised questions. Much has been said in the popular press about the so-called sexual or carnal nature of Tantra. Where does that view fit with the goals stated above?

The simple answer from an initiate is: Tantra is the science of celibacy.

At this point, some thrill-seekers may stop reading this chapter. But our statement is accurate. Tantra is the science of total inward absorption of energies. Let us understand here what constitutes sexual or other desires.

What are we? We each are a wave in the ocean of Consciousness. Waves may appear to be separate but try drawing a boundary line between two waves and we find out that it is one continuum. This wave, ray, beam of light passing through our psycho-physiological complex compound, is the "personal" *kuṇḍalinī*. It is the identity of all our energies, differentiated into its various functions.

These functions may be named (a) *cit-kuṇḍalinī* (the paths of pure consciousness), (b) *citta-kuṇḍalinī* (the paths of the mind flow), and (c) *prāṇa kuṇḍalinī* (the channels of *prāṇa*).

In Ayurveda, we are taught how these wave paths are distributed through the person's body in the form of three types of channels, *nāḍīs*, viz. (a) *mano-vaha* (the channels of mind's flow throughout the body), (b) *prāṇa-vaha* (same for *prāṇa*), and (c) *sroto-vaha* (the vessels for the flow of bodily essences). The subtler level *nāḍīs* control the progressively grosser levels of the same. Warps of consciousness and the mind produce the psycho-physiological warps. By the same token, all sensations in the body are manifestations of the presence of the *kuṇḍalinī* wave, however warped or diluted.

Here we digress to another question. Often a spiritual guide is asked: How do I find my way inwards to the spiritual realm? The answer from an experienced guide would be: The same way that you found your way outwards!

There are not two different doors for you to enter and exit your house, one designated for entry and the other for exiting. The same door through which you came out is the entryway. Thus every sense and every sensation is an entryway inwards to the spiritual realm. Every sensation in the body is a reminder of the presence of the *kuṇḍalinī* wave.

The spiritual energy wave flows outwards from its central core *bindu*. It energizes all levels and layers of our being. There is no energy in us except spiritual energy, transmuted into various grosser forms in order to fulfil certain purposes to keep this personalized self-running.

The charges of energy released from inside activate our senses. The impulses and sensations, thus produced, generate what we call desires. These desires are nothing but signals given by the *kuṇḍalinī:* I am here, I am here, I am here.

We do not recognize the signals and expend energy outwards in sensations of taste, touch, sight and so forth. Hence, the sexual act. Two (male and female) intertwine with one another, hoping thereby to become one again. But they will never succeed this way. The experience of gender and sex needs to be carefully examined. Bodily sensations should be treated as reminders, that here an entryway, a pathway inwards, exists. Take to that pathway and the inward wave carries you to the interior realm of non-duality beyond the pairs of opposites.

Tantra teaches how we may take our familiar sensations and reverse their flow inwards. Any stimulus must be used as an object of concentration to lead one inwards. There are few rare ones who have mastered this science, yet rarer ones who can actually teach it. They can enter *samādhi* by tasting a single sip of orange juice, or feeling the sensation from a tiny touch of a fingertip. For them, there is only one male in the universe, that is, Śiva; only one female, that is, Śakti. Such ones have total control over their *nāḍī*s, channels of awareness. They may choose to flow outwards at will, for example into instant poetry, if that will help liberate others, or they may enJOY themselves within. They need no external props, and all external props to them are stimuli to flow inwards.

Such ones dwell in an inward ecstasy. Their toes curl as they experience the upward flow of *kuṇḍalinī,* from the foundation-centre (*mūlādhāra*) to *Brahman*-opening (*brahma-randhra*). They become incapable of wasting their *bindu* (the drop of light) whether they are of male or female physical form. They have no interest in that three-second phenomenon when both nostrils flow simultaneously, which is the poverty-stricken experience during a sexual climax. The tāntric master's both nostrils flow evenly for hours naturally in the state of inward absorption, *laya.* No worldly sensation can compare with that state of bliss.

Those who have not gone through this process of transmuting the outward body sensations continuously waste the messages the *kuṇḍalinī* sends to our outer surfaces, by a cosmic whisper: I am *in* here, I am *in* here; come on *in!!* Why are you running out there mistaking a morsel of cake to be the source of your pleasure, the tiny touch of a bare skin to be the origin of your ecstasy? Come back *in.*

Listening to that message is Tantra.

What pleasure of sexual union can equal the state described in the tāntric text *Vijñāna-bhairava*:

svavad anya-śarīre 'pi samvittim anu-bhāvayet ।
apekṣam sva-śarīrasya tyaktvā vyapi dinair bhavet ॥

Cause the consciousness to be experienced in another body just as one experiences it in one's own. Then one is no longer dependent on one's own body and will have mastered pervasiveness within a few days.

If such a one gives someone an embrace, s/he transfers a sublime consciousness in the process, for there, only mind embraces mind. The embrace becomes an initiation. Alas, some unscrupulous persons claiming to be great teachers misunderstand the teaching, exploit their disciples for personal exterior pleasure, and call that Tantra!

Here we have explained the principle of Tantra as being the art of celibacy. I wish the monks and nuns of all religions did not have to struggle so much against desires, that they could all be taught this methodical art of celibacy. However, detailed methods for accomplishing this cannot be described here, nor can they be learned in a day. The first prerequisite to be considered a qualification for such a teaching (*adhikārin*) is a resolve to purity. Purity comes by the spiritual guide raking you over hot coals. Wish to run away from the *āśrama* of such a scrupulous guide? Go ahead. It is your loss.

There are certain misunderstandings also about the nature of *cakra*s.

Apart from all the multi-chrome, beautiful lotuses, which do indeed depict the higher meditational experiences of *cakra*s, what exactly are they?

Think of a high voltage cable running concealed in a wall, with many outlets for plugs. Connect a heater, a cooler, air conditioner, fan, TV, radio, recording apparatus through the different sockets. Each machine draws its power from the same cable. However, the power is transmuted into various forms of energy according to the purpose of the machine and its design. Power becomes heat in a heater or motion in a fan.

So it is with *kuṇḍalinī*. Different forms of psycho-physiological apparatuses are plugged into it. The one and only force is transmuted into various functions. As you read this chapter, close your eyes, mentally probe the region between your eyebrows, then the area of your throat, then the cardiac region, then the navel region, then, the *svādhiṣṭhāna* and *mūlādhāra* regions as well.

Impulses, feelings, sensations and desires at each place are experienced differently. The world seems to present very different faces to each of these centres of consciousness. At the eyebrow and forehead centre, it feels very different from the facet it presents to the heart centre, and so on. The same *kuṇḍalinī* diversifies into all these different interpretations of the world and helps us experience these different aspects and facets.

We also know intuitively the functions of these psycho-physiological centres. For deep thinking, we rub our foreheads. For expressing feelings, we place the hand on the chest.

Each *cakra*, as an above-stated energy centre, also controls the physical organs of the region. There are special meditations and concentrations — not popularly known — for helping correct psychological and physical handicaps and disorders associated with each of these regions.

One hears a great deal about "raising the *kuṇḍalinī*" and "opening the *cakra*s". Quite often, phenomena popularly associated with these highly spiritual levels of evolution are not what they seem to be. Here, we take three situations.

1. Involuntary movements in the body do not necessarily mean that one's *kuṇḍalinī* has been raised. Sometimes neuro-cerebral disorders mimic the *kuṇḍalinī* phenomena. Also the involuntary movements show

that the lower energy fields and channels have not yet been purified. It is the spiritual guide's duty to lead the disciple through necessary purifications, and when these have been accomplished, the one simple, single sign of the awakening of *kuṇḍalinī* is not involuntary movements, but total stillness of such a degree that a restless person coming in the presence of such an accomplished one may find his/her emotions and senses effortlessly stilled.

2. The same applies to the feelings of quasi-electrical sensations flowing through the channels of the personality. These sensations may be in the *prāṇa* and mind channels, and not necessarily in the *kuṇḍalinī* channels. If one truly wishes to make spiritual progress, one needs to be cautious about ego and false romanticism about these phenomena. One whose *kuṇḍalinī* is awakened is so pure that no one's anger touches him/her, nothing makes his smile fade; no matter what you do to him, there is no diminution of his universal and totally selfless love.

3. As to opening the *cakra*s, once again, a seeker needs to be cautious. Some popularizers of false Tantra make claims about the opening of, say, *svādhiṣṭhāna*, and equate it with much sexual activity. In fact, in the world of *śakti*s, *unmeṣa* is *nimeṣa* and *nimeṣa* is *unmeṣa;* that is, opening means closing and closing means opening. Opening of *cakra*s means closing their outward and downward gates and channels, and opening them inwards and upwards. Here are few of the symptoms of opening of *cakra*s.

A. *Mūlādhāra*: Its opening means:

a. one's meditation *āsana* has become stabilized. One may sit totally immobile for three hours or three days; this immobility must be totally effortless and relaxed.

b. A person whose *mūlādhāra* is awakened does not exhibit uncontrolled movements of the body and senses such as the eyes.

c. Everything in her/his surroundings becomes stabilized because s/he has dropped all emotional instability and insecurity.

B. One whose *svādhiṣṭhāna* is opened becomes truly and naturally celibate. S/he cannot waste the sexual energy downwards; the moment a physical sensation of sexual nature arises, it immediately ascends to the sixth *cakra* and produces there a tremendous quasi-electric implosion. All sexual sensation becomes an invitation to enter a state of meditation; the path of sensation is reversed, leads into the *suṣumṇā* channel, and thence to the higher centres of consciousness. Married *sādhaka*s also who are properly trained, sometimes receive initiation into such an upward path.

C. One whose *maṇipūra cakra* is open, masters the *prāṇa* fires. S/he can channel the *prāṇa* into whichever organ, to heal and energize oneself even when s/he is enfeebled by physical illness and fatigue through incessant service to others.

D. One whose *anāhata cakra* has opened has developed universal, selfless love for all. S/he needs no emotional support and fulfilment from others but becomes to them whatever they seek him/her to be, becomes everyone's support. Such a one also masters *yoga-nidrā*, produces delta brain waves at will, can learn any science in the state of conscious sleep.

E. One whose *viśuddha cakra* has opened goes into natural silence. If s/he were to speak, his/her words would reverberate around the planet for 1,000 years. Such a one has mastered the dream state and all creative processes in arts.

F. One whose *ājñā cakra* has opened receives the purest intuitive knowledge, which is not based on guesswork nor on logical processes. Such knowledge arises as a flash non-sequentially. By opening the *ājñā cakra*, one stands at the ladder to *guru-cakra, manas-cakra* and *sahasrāra*. Of these, we may write at another time.

The signs of the opening of *cakras* given above are only illustrative and not exhaustive. It is a subject for personal experience under guidance.

If a reader thinks s/he is ready now to pack his bags to get to an *āśrama* to have his/her *kuṇḍalinī* raised and to have the *cakra*s opened, it is not that simple. As we have stated above, a tremendous level of purification is required. For example, because Tantra requires veneration of Śakti, a true teacher of Tantra and Śri-vidyā will carefully observe a male disciple's attitudes towards women. The tāntric texts repeatedly and emphatically state that a student of Tantra and Śri-vidyā must pay utmost respect to women.

Here are some examples of the attitude and behaviour required.

A tantra-disciple must:

1. not be angry with anyone in the presence of a woman, leave alone being angry with a woman,
2. speak to women with great respect,
3. not criticize women in general and any woman in particular,
4. regard all females as incarnations of *śakti* and behave with them as with the Devī Herself,
5. not appear before a woman unkempt and looking disorderly, but should be well dressed and well groomed in their presence, and
6. regard a woman's entire being as pure and venerable.

Also,

1. If a woman is pleased with him, the Devī is pleased; if a woman is displeased, the Devī is displeased.
2. If one passes some women, strangers, standing and chatting, one should mentally bow and pay homage to them.

It is stated that no rules of purification and discipline are required of women and an initiation given by a woman teacher is ten or 100 times more effective.

Well, these are rules for men; what about women? They should recognize their *śakti*-being and grant grace and graciousness accordingly.

Bearing the above in mind, how many of us are ready for the teachings of Tantra?

It is obvious that if the teachings of Tantra were taken seriously, the world society, would be very different from what it is today. Let us hope that many can qualify to receive the teachings of Tantra and thereby truly realize that all mental habit patterns must be dropped in order to achieve liberation.

May all be Freed!

Swami Veda Bharati

1

Who Am I?

This contemplation was guided in Bremen, Germany, 1 May 2006.

As the audience sat entranced with the eyes closed, the meditative voice led each participant into experiencing the question and then the answer through observing the consciousness as source of the breathing process.

It is included here because the first knowledge of *kuṇḍalinī* is in the breath.

WHO am I? What am I? This is a question that every human being has asked at one time or another.

Let us contemplate on "who am I" and "what am I". Who is asking this question? Look inside your mind and see from where the question is arising. Before the words of the question form, a quiet, silent inquiry comes, deeper than the words of the question. Go to the place where the feeling of the question arises. It is that feeling that then looks for words.

Where is the seed of that feeling? To find that seed go into your pure consciousness. Consciousness here is not an abstract noun. It is a proper noun. It is your name. The only name you have. Consciousness is your only name. All other names are names of conditions imposed upon you.

You are the nameless consciousness that simply is, *asti*. It is to be experienced only as pure being. Simply be aware of being, free of names and conditions. Names of conditions of the body and its parts are not your names. You are pure being, being that is consciousness. Know yourself to be that.

You, the being that is consciousness, are not a composite of more than one element. Not being constituted of components, you were never born. Your composition will never dissolve into many composites. You will never die. You are from eternity to eternity. You are a being, a consciousness-being through whom the entire infinity passes. Know yourself to be that infinite consciousness-being.

Here and now, be aware only of your being, nameless, free of conditions. No conditions of delimitations of space and time apply to your being. Thus the sages have found within themselves. This is the self of the saintly beings. That very self you are. You are a pure, self-aware energy field. Around that pure energy field the conditioned matter builds a house. All conditions are conditions of that material house.

You, the pure consciousness energy-being, only dwell in that house. You are not the house. Conditions of the house are not your conditions: tall, short, giant, dwarf, male, female, foetus, infant, child, adolescent, youth, elderly. Your horizons are horizons of infinity. You are that.

Affirm in your mind: I am that (*so 'ham*) (pronounced *so hum*). For a few moments of deep silence feel yourself to be that infinite, conditionless, pure consciousness energy-being! Remain in the knowledge of being that.

You are the dweller of a material house. You are not the house. Remain aware of being the pure being even if you open the windows, the senses of your house. Remain the untouched indweller even when the sights, sounds, fragrances, tactile sensations enter the house.

Be the observer, controller, untouched, neutral witness. Then there is no sorrow, no grief for you, the pure being. Then in your infinity there are no expectations, no disappointments. Continuously reaffirm: I am that (*so 'ham*).

Know that it is your presence through whose touch this material house comes into life. Because you touch this material shape of the body, the body becomes a person. Because you send forth your consciousness wave, the mind establishes a semblance of awareness. Thus made aware, the mind as the subtlest, finest material energy, activates the mechanisms of the brain and the nervous systems. When you withdraw your consciousness wave, all the neural activities of the brain cease.

You are the pure, conditionless, infinite self that enlivens the mind, brain and the nerves. Know yourself to be that. Affirm to yourself: I am that (*so 'ham*).[1] Let not that affirmation be a verbal condition, for verbal conditions are temporary and time bound. You are the very self of infinity.

Do not state it to be inward or outward, only know yourself to be that and dwell in that self-knowledge of being the infinite field.

As such a one, infinite being of consciousness, you send forth a wave of your oceanic being. The wave touches the mind field. The mind field receives a semblance of awareness. The wave of the infinite life-force, that you are,

---

[1] To be pronounced *so-hummm*. So also wherever this *ham* occurs.

filters through the mind. Thus filtered through, the wave touches *prāṇa*, the field of vitality. The wave becomes a floating current of aliveness. And the person comes alive.

The mind and *prāṇa* consistently, continuously respond to this transcendental rhythm. These currents moving rhythmically create a harmonic, melodic music through the organs of your entire house. The universal music plays through all the instruments, the inner organs. Their rhythmic melody runs the entire body. That which would have been some trapped air in the cavities of these organs responds to that soft, gentle music. That which would have been some trapped air in the cavities of the body begins to flow as a soft, gentle stream.

That melodious, rhythmic stream you name as your breath. You breathe and you say: I am alive. Observe this stream of aliveness that you have named your breath all the way from the wave of infinite, life-force and consciousness filtering through the mind, touching the *prāṇa* field, energizing the internal organs into musical, harmonious, rhythmic movements, producing the externalized manifestation of the wave of consciousness called your breathing.

Observe this entire consciousness and life-force process of your breath stream. Know your breath stream to be a gift as a wave of infinity. Observe the musical, rhythmic movement of the organs which are producing this breath stream.

Observe the gentle rise and fall of your navel region, the seat of your *prāṇa*, that sends forth your breath stream.

Observe your breath channel from your navel to the nostrils and from the nostrils to your navel. Breathe slowly, gently, smoothly.

Observe your breathing; no jerk in your breathing. Let your breath be smooth and even like a prolonged musical note from a violin, without a break between two notes.

As you come to the end of the consciously observed exhalation, immediately come to the consciously observed inhalation.

As you complete one consciously observed inhalation without a pause, begin the next consciously observed exhalation, slow and gentle.

Remain aware of the wave of infinite consciousness and life-force that is sending forth the breath flow. Know yourself to be that: I am that (*so 'ham*).

Exhaling think: ham. Inhaling think: *so*.

Feel the flow and the touch of the breath in the nostrils with *so 'ham*.

As you exhale, it is your mind that exhales. As you inhale your breath returns to the seat of your mind. No break between the breaths. No break in the thought of *so 'ham*.

Know your breath to be a vehicle of that wave of infinity that you are. Resolve to walk in the world with this awareness, always remaining linked to the consciousness of that divinity which is your source, which is your current dwelling place, which is your place of total interior rest.

May all the saints of all religions, the saints of no religions, all prophets, all *boddhisattva*s and *buddha*s, all liberated beings, the founders of the *guru* lineages and of our own *guru* tradition — all one in infinite divinity — bless you with that peace whose very self you infinitely are.

I suggest that for today you rise from your reading in silence. Maintain this awareness as long as you can, go to sleep with this awareness so that you may awaken with the divine light within you. I invite you to dip daily in that holy Ganges of infinity that flows within you.

2

Why Yogīs Choose Celibacy?[1]

> All the *cakras* are held in the *sahasrāra* (the thousand-petalled lotus). The *sahasrāra* is held in the spiritual heart (*hṛdaya*) (*dahara ākāśa* = infinite expanse of inner space, hidden in the minute cavern of the heart). *Hṛdaya* (*dahara ākāśa*) is held in *suṣumṇā*. *Suṣumṇā* is held in *śūnya* (Eternal Void). *Śūnya* is held in *Paramātman* (Supreme Self). *Paramātman* is held in *Parabrahman* (the transcendent Pure Being). — Vamadeva Shastri

LET us begin with the question of the origin of the sexes. Socrates held that in some Golden Age each of us was a single, united being — that the masculine and the feminine were equally present in every person — but that somewhere along the line a fall occurred and the two aspects separated, and that ever since then, females and males have been searching for their counterparts.

This is very similar to some of the words we read in the traditions of India. Consider, for example, the following passage from a great Sanskrit epic, *Kumāra-sambhava* (2.3-15) of Kālidāsa:

> Then they [the gods] fell before Him, the Sustainer of all, the Lord of Speech with faces in all directions; they

---

[1] Previously published in *Dawn*, vol. 3 no. 1, 1983 under the title, *The Spiritual Nature of Sexuality*.

> stood addressing Him with words filled with depths of meanings:
>
> Salutations to You of three forms, the Absolute One Self before creation, Who then became divided, apportioning the three attributes of Nature.
>
> As You sowed the unfailing seed in the waters and from that arose the moving and unmoving things of the world, You are glorified as its source, O Unborn One.
>
> Though One, You emanate Your power through three conditions, having become the cause of dissolution, maintenance and creation.
>
> Man and woman are Your two halves as You split Your form with intent to create: they are then the birth-givers of the creation and are called its parents.

Similarly, we read in the ancient Lawbook of Manu:

> It was all turned dark, not recognizable, without marks, unanalysable, unknowable, as though asleep all over.
>
> [*Compare Genesis 1.2:* And the earth was without form and darkness was upon the face of the deep.]
>
> Then the Self-Existent Being, the Lord, unmanifest, manifesting all elements and so forth, with His power activated, appeared, the dispeller of darkness.
>
> He Who is beyond the grasp of the senses, subtle, unmanifest, eternal, Who is one with all beings, beyond thought — the very One Self shone forth.
>
> Intent on creating the various progenies from His own body, having meditated, He first created the very (cosmic) waters: and released His seed upon them.
>
> That became a golden egg with the splendour of a

thousand suns. In that was born Brahmā Himself, the Creator, the grandfather of all the worlds.

[*Compare Genesis 1.7:* And God made the firmament and divided the waters.]

The (cosmic) waters are called Nara (pronounced *nārā*), for they are the child of Nara the Cosmic Person, the Lord. Since He first dwelt upon them, therefore He is called Nārāyaṇa.

[*Compare Genesis 1.2:* And the Spirit of God moved upon the face of the waters.]

That which is the Eternal, Unmanifest Cause, comprising both being and non-being, created by that One, the (Cosmic) Person is called Brahmā[2] in the world.

Having dwelt in that (golden) egg for a year, the Lord, through the meditation of His own Self, divided that egg twofold.

Dividing His body into two, He became a male by one half and by the other half a female. In her the Master created Virāṭ [the unitary principle of the cosmos of multiple phenomena.]

So, the tradition from within which we speak here has this original unity of the male and the female principles.

Now let us shift the ground from the universal male and universal female to the male and the female within ourselves.

There is a figure in India known as Śiva, who is often depicted as half male and half female — called the Ardha-

[2] The two words, *Brahman* and Brahmā are not to be confused. The former is the transcendental formless one, the latter is the emanent Cosmic Person.

nārīśvara, the Lord or the Lady, as you wish. However, it is not the same idea as that of hermaphrodite, because we are speaking here of a spiritual principle and not of physical appearances. We are speaking not of an abnormal duality but of a perfect or divine state in which opposites are in a complementary union.

This brings us to the area of Tantra. This word has become very exciting to some people. Much is written on Tantra, but the popular literature abounds in distortions and misrepresentations. People do not really understand Tantra. Tantra is the science of celibacy.

One who understands Tantra fully becomes a natural celibate.

In Tantra, we speak of the force called *kuṇḍalinī*. Briefly, it is not that there is a force called *kuṇḍalinī* in us: rather, *kuṇḍalinī* is the very stream of divine consciousness from which the entire personality emanates, from which all the energies of our personality are generated.

In fact, this entire universe is a dance of energies. There is nothing else in the universe but a dance of energies. At some point the energies split into conscious energies and unconscious energies and a certain dichotomy occurs: a certain duality out of the unity evolves. We read in the Upaniṣads:

He was One, alone.
He knew, He saw, "I am alone".
He said. "Let me become many; let me progenitize".

Again and again the same theme occurs:

Thereby, He split Himself into two.

The non-self-aware energies in and of the universe are called nature; the conscious energies are called God, soul, *kuṇḍalinī*. The universal energy of consciousness plugged into us is called the *kuṇḍalinī*.

Three beings unite, and a conception takes place. Who are the three beings? The mother, the father, and the soul who is to be born. It is not that two beings unite and conception takes place. Two beings can keep uniting a million times without conception occurring. Three beings must unite for conception to occur.

So this stream of energy enters and an embodied being comes into existence. This process is analogous to what happens when iron filings come in contact with a magnet. If a magnet is placed under a piece of paper and then some iron filings are sprinkled on the paper, the iron filings move and arrange themselves in the shape of the magnetic field. Similarly, this human body with its symmetry, with its proportional arrangements, with its north and south poles, with all of its forms perfectly balanced — split in half, as it were, left side and right side, this body is arranged along the lines of the energy field called the *kuṇḍalinī*.

The pathways of the *kuṇḍalinī* are very clearly visible. Look at the central hairline. If you observe the body's hairline, you see the arrangement of the *kuṇḍalinī*. Everything in the body is arranged along the force field of the *kuṇḍalinī*.

In the *kuṇḍalinī*, in the stream of consciousness, there is neither male nor female; rather, there are both male and female, as in the universe there is nothing purely masculine, nothing purely feminine.

The masculine and the feminine are interposed upon each other. You look at something in one mood, one sentiment, one emotion, one place, it is very feminine. You look at that very thing in a different mood, in a different place, in a different context, it is very masculine. The river flows: very feminine. The floodgates open: very masculine. All these are our interpretations of the feminine and the masculine. In the same way, there is no human being who is purely feminine, who is purely masculine. In us both are united.

The *kuṇḍalinī* force that is plugged in us, as it were, is at present not in its full glory, but concealed, covered, enmeshed in bad conductors of energy, because we have not developed our inward consciousness.

The stream of the *kuṇḍalinī* has no direction upwards, nor downwards, neither in front nor behind. But if we look at it in body terms, it flows from the base of the spine to the top of the head. This is also the site of the core of our nervous system, but the *kuṇḍalinī* is not to be identified as one with the nervous system. The *kuṇḍalinī* is not gauged by the pulses of the nerves, but rather is itself the cause and source of the energy of the nervous system. This *kuṇḍalinī*, this stream of consciousness, is described by the great *yogī*s as being like a constant, unbroken flash of lightning, slim as one ten-thousandth of a hairs breadth, shining with the brilliance of ten thousand suns. We read in *Saundaryalaharī*:

> slim as a streak of lightning,
> comprising of sun, moon and fire.

Thus the *kuṇḍalinī* is described: the light of the soul flowing from the base of the spine to the top of the head. If you think of it only as a spine, it's like a rod. If you see the energy in it, it becomes a snake. Therefore we read in the Bible Moses asking the Lord, "How will my people be convinced that You have truly visited me?" God replies, "Cast the rod". Moses does so, and the rod becomes a snake. Moses at that point has the awakening of the *kuṇḍalinī*: the rod becomes a snake.

When the snake falls into the lower realms, then what happens? The arch-angel falls into the subterranean regions: paradise lost. Read in Milton, the story of the fall of the *kuṇḍalinī*. In *Paradise Lost* the arch-angel rebels and falls into the regions below the earth and remains confined to the fires therein. It is thus that our innocence is lost. The fallen *kuṇḍalinī* comes to Eve and she is tempted by the snake: "Eat this fruit of the experience of good and evil in the world." She succumbs. Until then there is no nakedness; until then there is no sexuality.

When the *swāmī*s take the vow of swāmīhood, from that moment they are considered, ideally, genderless. A monk is likewise neither male nor female. So also in the Catholic tradition, a nun is the bride of Christ. Only the virgin, the pure *kuṇḍalinī*, not touched by the stains of the earth, is capable of giving birth to saintliness, Christ-consciousness.

As this *kuṇḍalinī* flows like a thrill from the base of the spine to the top of the head, at certain points along the line it sends forth tiny pulses. The *kuṇḍalinī* can be viewed as a vertical flow of energy from the base of the spine to the top of the head, with spaced horizontal pulses being generated. Where these horizontal pulses are being sent out, there certain psycho-physiological vortices occur. Where the *kuṇḍalinī* is producing the pulses, there, in combination with our mind-force, *prāṇa*-force, and physical reality, the psycho-physiological vortices occur.

Because of that pulse being sent into the psycho-physiological vortex, a certain aliveness occurs there. So the organs in that region pulsate and begin to function. As this happens, all kinds of sensations are felt in those regions because of the energy that is present. As these organs begin to move in response to the pulses that are sent forth in harmony with the pulse and rhythm of the whole universe through that pulsation, through the rhythmic movement of these organs — that which would have been some stale air trapped in some cavities becomes a flowing breath.

Thus the embodied being comes alive.

By our *karma* we must fulfil certain aspects of life in the feminine genre. By our *karma* we must fulfil certain aspects of life in the masculine genre. The genre becomes the gender. Certain things we can do only in a feminine body; certain other things we can do only in a masculine body. Certain things we can do only in a predominantly feminine psyche, certain other things we can do only in a predominantly masculine psyche. Therefore, by that *karma* we are born either a male or a female. But there remains within each of us a very conscious knowledge that we are incomplete by being merely masculine or by being merely feminine. We must complete ourselves.

Because we are in the habit of directing our attention outward, we search for completion in the exterior world: if we are female we look for a male, if we are male we look for a female, hoping to unite with that counterpart of ours of whom Socrates spoke. We are like the musk deer: in the Himalayas there is a legend that at a certain time in the right season the smell of musk from the navel of the musk deer is so strong that the deer goes crazy looking all around for the source of this wonderful fragrance, running here and there on the mountain peaks searching for the source of the odour.

But the *yogī* who knows Tantra turns his gaze inward. He knows that masculinity and femininity share a single source, and that a complete person is both masculine and feminine. Thus, as one grows spiritually, especially on the path of the *kuṇḍalinī,* the outward search turns inward and one's personal qualities change.

There is much popular misunderstanding concerning *kuṇḍalinī* and *cakra*s. People think that someone whose throat *cakra* is opened will talk a lot, one whose heart *cakra* is opened will become exceedingly emotional, one whose pelvic *cakra* is open will over-indulge in sexual act, and so forth. That is not the way.

The opening of the *cakra*s means the closing of all outward symptoms.

One whose throat *cakra* opens becomes naturally silent.

One whose heart *cakra* opens does not go through fits of crying and laughing and other such emotional outbursts, but rather becomes possessed of an unshakable stability of emotion. Such a person's love will be all-encompassing, but he or she will not go through fits and turmoils of emotionalism.

One whose pelvic *cakra*s open becomes naturally celibate.

Why? Because we flow inwards and upwards when we meditate and when our *cakra*s open.

Even in the dormant state of the *kuṇḍalinī,* when we say the *kuṇḍalinī* is not awake, and the *cakra*s are not open, how much energy there is! Think, for instance, of all that our head does and has done. Or simply try to imagine all the communication going on now all over the planet: radio programmes, television broadcasts, lectures, movies, conversations, parties and so on. So here at our fingertips, at our heart centre, in our sexual organs, in our throat region — at the moment we have all these activities going on.

If any more energy was released into these vortices, what would we do with it? If more energy were to flow outwards from these *cakras*, where would be the sluice gate for that floodgate?

Look at our hearts: if there were more energy flowing out that way, would we be able to handle it? Or consider the sexual region: the little that the *kuṇḍalinī* sends into this area keeps an average person dizzy with all kinds of thoughts, fantasies, desires and indulgences. If we had more energy flowing into there, would there be any law and order in the world?

The meditator turns the flow of energy inward. The *yogī* goes into meditation and says, "Ah yes, this sensation, now, where does it come from?" In fact, in meditation the energy rises and becomes intensified. There are periods in the practices of *kuṇḍalinī* in which the disciple experiences a marked increase in the level of crypto-sexual energy, but if the student is under the guidance of a qualified *guru*, then the *guru* explains that this is not sexual arousal, it is simply the intensification of energy, and instructs the disciple to trace the sensation to its source. Then through special breathing practices, concentration exercises and meditations that are done in *kuṇḍalinī-yoga*, the practitioner goes to the interior source of these pulsations.

From the psycho-physiological vortex the *yogī* goes to the pulse that has impulsated the vortex; riding that pulse he goes to the thrill of the *kuṇḍalinī*. When he has learned to trace this pathway, that very intensification of energy that a moment ago was trilling in the lower parts of the personality — or in any given parts of the body — is taken inward and bursts through a point up in the seventh heaven: the arch-angel rises again. But, to accomplish this, the practitioner must be under the guidance of a qualified *guru* who knows how to help the student establish control and can give the right techniques for drawing the energy inward and upward.

This is not to say, however, that if a person wants to make progress on the path of *kuṇḍalinī-yoga* s/he has to take a vow of celibacy. There have been thousands of married *yogī*s in the traditions. It all depends on a number of factors.

In fact, the first thing that happens through *yoga* is the intensification of sensual pleasure. You see, if we want to enjoy our senses, we have to learn the art of enjoying. We do not know the art of enjoying our senses because we indulge in them in random ways. We have not learned that there are only two sources of enjoyment: restraint and concentration.

In any aesthetic activity, whether it be painting or music or sexual indulgence (which is an aesthetic activity as appreciation of beauty), the source of pleasure is in restraint and concentration. It is not possible, for instance, to play or enjoy music without restraint and without concentration.

Whatever a person wants to concentrate on is pleasure; whatever a person wants to concentrate away from is pain.

The greater the concentration, the greater the pleasure. A person on the path of *yoga* knows to enjoy the senses through that concentration much more than someone who has not learned the art of concentration.

But the tragedy with our prevalent sensual attitudes is this: we think that the more often we engage in sensual pleasure, the more pleasure we will have. Some think that the more sexual partners they have, the more pleasure they will have. But it is through conservation that concentration develops. Restraint gives us intensity.

When you have that intensity, don't spend it in one short moment. Through that very restraint go slowly: give your concentration time. Then it is not possible for a man and a woman to become bored with each other. Human beings are an immensely rich treasure, each man and each woman. Discover the riches with restraint and concentration.

If you engage in marital union only with the unselfish thought of giving the loving gift of pleasure to your partner, you are as good as a celibate. If you indulge only for a moment's personal release, you are merely a loser of energy. Unselfishness, coupled with a meditative life, will teach you to draw inward, even from the most sensually attractive engagements. That's the next step. You will then look to the source of your pleasure, and you will find it in the *kuṇḍalinī*.

The ecstasy of sex is infinitesimal compared to the ecstasy of the *yogī* in *samādhi*.

It is not that the *yogīs* are saying that your sex is sinful or that it is not pleasant for you; but they are saying that they have discovered a pleasure that is a million times more intense, known as *ānanda*. This is the difference between the *yogī* and the puritan. What is experienced in sex is only a tiny taste of something infinitely more full. Go to that, and you will have eternal union of the male and the female within you.

The split is healed; the prime One is re-discovered. An eternal ecstasy ensues.

It is for that reason that the *yogī* becomes celibate and lives in *ānanda*.

*Yogī*s are the true pleasure seekers.

3

Emotion Centres in Meditation

THIS chapter is an answer in two parts of a single question related to the experience of celibacy and passionate desires in the course of one's spiritual and meditative life.

The first part of the question addresses the understanding and application of words like "libido", "desire", "celibacy" and "sublimation". What do these words mean?[1]

Why is there always such a controversy and conflict between the question of sexuality and spirituality, sexuality and religion?

Why have so many spiritual paths throughout history considered the life of celibacy to be sacred? The Greek and the Roman virgin goddesses, virgin prophetesses, Vestal Virgins of Rome, Catholic nuns, Indian *swāmīs*, Buddhist monks and nuns, all, have embraced celibacy. Even during the *hajj*, the sacred pilgrimage to Mecca, it is prohibited to become *ham-bistar* (sharing a bed). *What* is the reason for such a universal reverence for celibacy?

---

[1] For more information, please ask for (1) recordings of Five Silences Seminar, given on 12 February 1977 (cassette #77002), (2) Five Pillars of *Sādhanā*, and (3) Song of Silence, Subtleties in *Sādhanā*, all available from info@themeditationcentre.org or ahymsinpublishers @gmail.com.

Why, in all ages in all the lands, among the Taoist monks, among the American Indian people, are there periods of celibacy? There has been the tradition of virgin prophetesses among the American Indians. In Voodoo, periods of celibacy are prescribed for self-purification. When did the people of all these faiths and religions have a conference and agree upon this one ideal?

And, why is there such a rebellion against it today? The rebellion has arisen because that ideal is not understood. The period of the last 150+ years in the Western civilization (a minor portion of the history of world religions) is unlike any other period in the history of any other part of the world. In the concepts of civilization developed and being followed during this one-and-a-half century such disproportionate emphasis is placed on survival, passing on of genes. Every aspect of civilization sings the song only of body, body, body —nothing beyond.

Freud spoke of the underlying drive of libido, but what exactly is that libido? He explains its functions in our shallow levels of psychology, but what exactly is its origin, and what is its nature?

Then, nowadays we have all these "wonderfully exciting" Tantra books in the market. Hundreds of thousands of people buy them because they think that these would somehow explain what the people are struggling with; but they don't. They take people in a completely opposite direction.

It is not a question of sin and transgressions. It is a question of understanding the very source of our drives and urges.

An oft-recited verse in Sanskrit says that human beings have these four urges in common with all the animals: food, sleep, fear and aggression — for which only one word is used — fear that is aggression; aggression that is fear, and the sexual urge. Swami Rama called them the Four Fountains.

But *dharma*, the urge to virtue and righteousness, the urge to an interior spiritual discovery is unique to human beings. We need to understand these Four Fountains in terms of that other urge, the urge to *dharma*.

The present-day schools of psychology, by and large, with some exceptions, only deal with these four urges, taking them for granted. They simply are there — no rhyme or reason — their source is not understood; their spiritual origin is not explored. How these may be channelled into fulfilling the urge to *dharma* is hardly ever mentioned. What are these four, and why do we want to sublimate these four urges and make them tools for the realization of our other drive, the drive towards spirituality?

The above is the first part of the question. Directly related to that is the second part.

Many *sādhakas* (*sādhaka* in singular) and *sādhikās* are hesitant to ask this question out of modesty. Some are frank enough with their meditation guide, knowing fully that they will not be misunderstood.

What is the question? It comes in several versions:

Version 1: Lately, during meditation I experience tremendous sexual arousal. What is happening? What should I do?

Version 2: For some time now I have been finding myself thinking too many sexual thoughts, with very strong desires, during day and night. This is especially so during meditation but at other times as well.

Version 3: I came to your weekend meditation (*sādhanā*) retreat. It was wonderful. But I found myself indulging in tremendous sexual thoughts during the retreat. I am not normally that way. What happened to me? What should I do about it?

Version 4: Since I have started meditating seriously, my sexual drive has diminished and I am worried that it may make my spouse feel unhappy. Should I stop meditating for the sake of his/her happiness?

The questions are not limited to the meditation practitioners only. They are also asked by some practitioners of *haṭha-yoga* who practise the *āsana*s with awareness and breath synchronization — which are early stages of meditation also.

To understand this phenomenon, a seeker must comprehend the innermost constituent of human personality, known as the *kuṇḍalinī*. There is much misunderstanding about this term, and some thrill-seekers think of sexual energy as synonymous with *kuṇḍalinī*, which is far from the case.

Here, I recommend

1. Swami Rama's article, "The Awakening of *Kuṇḍalinī*", in the book on the same subject,[2]
2. Swami Muktananda's article in the same volume, and

---

[2] *Kuṇḍalinī, Evolution and Enlightenment*, ed. John White, Anchor Books/Doubleday, Garden City, New York (1979).

3. Swami Veda Bharati's recordings on *kuṇḍalinī* and *cakras*.[3]

All on the spiritual path speak of divinity within the human personality. Its mechanism is not well understood. Most briefly stated here, it is as follows:

There is a Sun called *parama-ātman*, Supreme Self; let us not, in order to placate some, call it by the currently outdated name "God"(!). One ray of this that has penetrated into our person-world is called *kuṇḍalinī*. It penetrates through the layers of *buddhi* (faculty of wisdom),[4] *manas* (mind), *prāṇa* (vital energy) and finally to our physiology. For those who understand *yoga* terminology, these are the layers through which this ray has to pass. That is how our entire personality becomes sentient and charged with consciousness and vitality.

It is thus that *kuṇḍalinī* runs all our psycho-physiological mechanisms. The same one ray of the Sun is divided into numerous rays, channels, *nāḍīs*: three, fourteen, one lakh,[5] one hundred and twenty-five thousand, thirty-five million. There are as many as that mentioned in the Tantra texts, but don't ask us here to recite the names of all thirty-five million branches of the *kuṇḍalinī*. Each level inwards is increasingly subtler. The entire network permeates our personality like an electronic grid. The number of channels depends on into how much subtlety one's meditation has

---

[3] Available from info@themeditationcentre.org and ahymsinpublishers@gmail.com.

[4] For deeper understanding of this faculty, read Swami Veda Bharati's *Commentary on the Yoga-sutras*, 2 vols., available from ahymsinpublishers@gmail.com.

[5] Hindi term for one hundred thousand.

gone. The science of this grid is called Tantra, which literally means "a grid".

The channels of this grid cross and criss-cross. Where two channels cross, it is called a *sandhi*, that is the technical term, or a "joint"; but not a joint such as between the bones. Where three channels cross, it is called a *granthi*, which means a "knot". Where more than three channels cross, it is called a *cakra*. The word *cakra* is linguistically cognate to the English words "circle" and "circus", as in "Oxford Circus" or "Piccadilly Circus", all part of a tremendously powerful circuit.

We are nothing but this circuit of the rays of God.

There are innumerable *cakra*s in this circuitry but seven main ones are commonly cited for beginners. These *cakra*s are the locations of the infusion and manifestation of divine energy into our psycho-physiological systems. The rays are infused into our psycho-physiological systems. It is like a powerful wire from the electrical mains into which numerous instruments are plugged: a water heater, a space heater, a refrigerator, a TV set, a fan and what not. All these instruments are run on the same power, but each one performs a different function depending on the tools and parts provided for heating, cooling and so on.

If the same circuit is connected to the psycho-physiological systems in the navel centre, it produces one power and one particular kind of function, one particular type of an urge — one particular kind of desire runs one particular complex of organs. If that electric wire is linked from inside to the heart centre, whatever instrumentation is there, then the energy takes that form, just as the same electric current can run a heater and a cooler both, depending upon the instrumentation.

In each *cakra* the *buddhi, manas, prāṇa,* charged by the rays of *kuṇḍalinī,* activate different sets of physical organs. So, each organ complex is connected to our different emotions on one hand, and to the physiology on the other.

The emotions you feel in, let us say, organs of the

- pelvic-perineal region,
- navel region,
- cardiac plexus,
- throat centre,
- *ājñā cakra* (eyebrow centre), and
- cerebral region

the *kuṇḍalinī* infused into these imparts power to emotions that function in these different organs. The same one power is distributed into these different forms — on one hand, the emotional power, on the other hand, the physiological function of those organs, thus forming a psycho-physiological complex. So we have a special emotional relationship with the organs, and the organs have a relationship with specific emotions.

Over thirty-five years ago I was teaching a course on the constituents of personality at our meditation centre in Minneapolis, USA. I asked if there was an artist in the audience. One young lady raised her hand.

I asked her to come forward and draw the outline of a human figure on the blackboard. She drew the outline. Then I said, "Now, looking at this outline, as an artist, where it feels balanced to your eye, place a dot there." So she placed a dot. Again I asked, "Now looking at the outline and the dot, again, wherever it looks balanced, place another dot." So she did. In this way I had her place, one after another, seven dots within the figure. I asked, "Have you ever heard of *cakra*s or seven centres of consciousness?" She replied, "No." I told her and the audience that the seven dots were exactly at the locations of the seven *cakra*s.

This episode also tells us of the deep intuitive knowledge we already have of the spiritual faculties within us. It takes only a little prompting to be discovered.

This also shows how the source of all art is intuition. And what is intuition? Knowledge of ourselves. You know how you are balanced internally, so you will draw a human figure that will be balanced.

The power of the physical organs plugged into these dotted points of power, these complexes, comes from the *kuṇḍalinī* circuitry. But the surface power that we experience in our emotions and urges and in the functioning of our organs is not even a drop of the dynamic ocean of energy that *kuṇḍalinī* is.

Naturally, when our power of concentration increases through meditation, the overall experience of energy in all of the organ-complexes — emotional energy, the energy manifested in the form of our urges and the physiological functioning of those organs — intensifies. A *yogī* can sit down and eat ten loaves of bread if he chooses to, but is he such a fool as to try it? He can also fast for 100 days without feeling an urge to consume, simply by concentrating on the energies in the hunger-emotion centre among the *cakra*s.

The *kuṇḍalinī* energy, when tapped, may become

- intensive effectiveness in all endeavours,
- tremendous intellectual power,
- inspired and flowing speech,

- the power of poetry or other arts,
- depth of silence,
- immense universal love into whose field is caught anyone who walks into the *yogī*'s presence,
- canine hunger, as was just described, or
- increased sexual urge if the *yogī* has not yet fully mastered the passion–emotion centres of consciousness, and so on.

A wise disciple under a *sad-guru* (a noble highly-qualified *guru*) will understand that these are only sparks of *kuṇḍalinī* that have become intensified.

Here we digress a moment into a different metaphor.

*Cakra*s, again, are where more than any three of the thirty-five million channels of *kuṇḍalinī* may meet. There is a *cakra* in index finger tip, and a *cakra* in the ring fingertip, and between the two nostrils (*nāsāgre*), and at the tip of the tongue. At the middle of the tongue, the root of the tongue where tongue may touch the roof of the mouth, as in *khecarī-mudrā*, there are *cakra*s. The *yogī*s use these *cakra*s for different purposes.

These *cakra*s are as gates that may open outwards or inwards.

Opening the *cakra*s means

closing the *cakra*s,

closing off their outward flow and diverting their intensive energy into the inward flow. Most worldly people make themselves into ever-leaking sieves through whose every sense-door the energy oozes, rushes and gushes outwards. The *yogī* interprets the sensations in the related senses and organs very differently.

The *yogī* knows that sexual feeling is placed in certain organs only to make us know that here is an energy complex, that it's a power house that you can tap for intensifying the upward flow and penetrating through the fog of delusion. It is now intensifying. Turn its flood inwards and it will become the inward penetrating power of intense meditation.

When the *sādhaka* encounters such an increased output of energy in any *cakra*, under no circumstances should one interpret it as a sexual desire or an impulse to indulge. S/he then needs to take it

- as a blessing,
- as an invitation to turn the flow inwards, and for that
- to practise the right attitudes, shift in emotion to convert the physical into spiritual and, again for that
- to practise the locks (*bandhas*) and seals (*mudrās*) that may be prescribed, together with
- the special techniques that the guide may show to make the energy flow inwards and upwards.

Some of these special techniques are:

- *Mūla-bandha* (root lock)
- *Aśvinī-mudrā*
- *Agni-sāra* (which has many levels, the subtlest one of which is the most effective but needs to be taught by an experienced expert)
- Concentrating on the breath flow between *maṇī-pūra* and *ājñā cakra*, with one's personal *mantra* (but the correct way of diaphragmatic and even breathing is its prerequisite)

- and other methods that cannot be mentioned here as they must be received by way of initiation.

It is also to be observed that with the awakening of the *kuṇḍalinī* the above "techniques" cease to be learned techniques but arise naturally in the *sādhaka's* person.[6]

When such an arisen energy is absorbed, it intensifies one's inward momentum and helps one penetrate through the various *kośa*s (sheaths), ultimately leading to *bindu-bhedana* (bursting through the point in the centre of the highest *cakra*).

In addition, even for normally outward-looking (*bahir-mukha*) people when one feels an awakening of sexual desire, that is the best time to enter into meditation. Then the meditation will be intense and deeply penetrating.

There is nothing more beautiful than spouses meditating together.

Along the way to this inward (*antar-mukha*) flow one must learn to contain all ecstasies and convert them into channels on the pure path (*śukla* or *śuddha pantha*).

For some people this energy that rises becomes a movement or an urge to dance or an uncontrollable crying or laughter. All that leakage, all of that outward rushing and gushing of energy is to be taken back in and made to flow along this very subtle channel.

Some are very fortunate because of the practices mastered in a previous life. They do not feel the restlessness caused by the awakening in the *cakra*s. Their awakened energy naturally flows towards the sublime.

[6] For details see this author's *Philosophy of Hatha Yoga*. One can understand this chapter, if one has grasped the contents of that book.

However, in case of householders, they need to learn the art of giving the spouse full satisfaction in love without losing one's own awakened energy. There are special ways to learn that — until such time that both partners can join subtle bodies and realize that the ecstasies experienced in the union of physical bodies were a mere foretaste of the far more powerful pleasure in the subtle world.

The *Yoga-Sūtras* of Patañjali warn against becoming attached even to the ecstasies of the subtle world so that one may go on beyond.

What has been said above also answers other related questions like, "Since I have started meditating I have been feeling the arousal of anger". Anger is also a warping of energy, and this warp needs to be unravelled by practices similar to the ones stated above, plus the re-training of emotions through *japa* and the four *brahma-vihāra*s — literally "the frolicking in God" of which we have spoken elsewhere.

This chapter will have explained to the *sādhaka*s what is the meaning of the word "libido", what is its origin, its nature, and what is it for. Also, then, why in all parts of the world, seemingly independently, wherever people have sought any spiritual solace, they have been taught the path of sublimation and have honoured virgins and celibates, who become prophets, monks, nuns, or even temporarily pilgrims whose pilgrimage becomes effective for them.

4

Body Movements, Symptom of Meditation?

ONE often encounters the phenomenon of many kinds of involuntary body movements during meditation.

They may be in the form of

- a to-and-fro or sideways swaying, or a circular or spiral-like motion,
- or even more drastic jerky motions of the body.

Often it may not be a physical movement but just a feeling.

Sometimes these movements occur

a. in the presence of an altar at a sacred place, with or without some ritual or liturgy, or

b. at a spot where a great *yogī* has performed *tapasyā* (ascesis, see *Yoga-Sūtra* 2.1) in the past left a *prasādam*[1] of energy whereby the place becomes sacred, charged, so as the visitors/pilgrims may receive such *prasādam* even for centuries to come.

---

[1] In the traditions of Hindu-Buddhist Asia, one makes offerings of food and other objects to a divine presence, sacred icon, spiritual guide or an elder. After it has been accepted as the offering, a portion is granted to the devotee as flow of grace which is received in the same spirit in which the holy wafer is received in the Christian tradition.

c. Some rivers or other bodies of water, or hilltops or caves, and such other natural spots, may be similarly charged and become centres of pilgrimage.

Such manifestation of energy may be invoked through

a. simply being "there" at that spot
b. through prayer at the sacred place
c. by reverently bowing to/at the holy ground.
d. It may also occur during one's personal meditation, in anyone of the forms of motion, physical or imaginary.

What exactly is this motion? What forces cause it? What is one advised to do about it?

Human beings enjoy responding to any out-of-the-ordinary experience. They respond with fear or joy or just excitation, or even in the form of vanity:

> Oh, look, how advanced I am. I sway during meditation. My *kuṇḍalinī* must be awake. Am I now a medium of the ancient *guru*s? May I now declare myself a great master and start granting grace and blessing and initiations?

There is even another form of vanity:

> I have a well charged energy in me. I can make people sway and jerk by awakening their energies.

In this brief presentation we shall attempt to understand what these phenomena are and what is one advised to do when they present themselves.

Having read the writings suggested in the last chapters, it should now be easy to understand the phenomenon but let us view it here succinctly.

A living being is a bundle of layers upon layers of energy fields wrapped one upon the other. These often remain dormant, wrapped by the sheets of *tamas* in the un-awakened beings. A little stir in this sleep, the *mudha*[2] state of our awareness, may take many forms.

There are many different networks of energy channels in our personality systems. Some of these are:

> channels of the *kuṇḍalinī*, meridians in the Chinese Chi system (utilized in acupuncture etc.),
>
> three kinds of channels taught in Ayurveda, namely, *mano-vaha* (those through which the mind flows), *prāṇa-vaha* (those through which *prāṇa* flows) and *śroto-vaha* (through which body fluids and hormones flow), and channels of mind *prāṇa*-composite energies used by teachers of many systems like Rei-ki, based on *Atharvaveda*. — 4.13.6-7

Which of the layers of our energy fields is being stirred in any experience of

- the presence of an external stimulus,
- sense experience,
- response thereto in the form of
  - emotion,
  - voluntary action
  - involuntary motion

OR

in the event of a wave of commonly dormant energy rippling within the constituents of our personality as a result of

---

[2] See commentary on *Yoga-Sūtras* 1.1 about five states of the mind-field.

- being touched by a powerful presence, or
- as a result of a break in the dormancy through
  - *sattva*-dominated *rajas* of the force field in a sacred place,
  - in a sacred presence,
  - or, again, a stirring of the *sattva*-dominated *rajas* of energies in meditation?

Yes, which of the layers is being stirred can be determined only by a Master.

How such a stir, which is in the nature of someone deeply asleep stirring a little or turning on his/her side, may be controlled, channelled, is also known only to a Master.

The primary questions to ask in determining our spiritual progress are not:

- Do I get stirred?
- Do I experience involuntary motion?

The questions to ask are:

- Do I become still?
- Does my presence grant stillness to others?

The genuine symptom of a spiritual experience is stillness through *sattva*, not motion through un-channelled *rajas*.

Once again, the question to ask is not: Do I get stirred?

The question to ask is: Do I get stilled?

There are three kinds of bodies in meditation:

- those that sweat (not be confused with those that feel a heat and can absorb it),
- those that move and sway, and

- those that become still.

The first two are those who

- have not yet purified their emotions,
- have not aligned the *prāṇa* bodies, and
- have not prepared their body-vessels to be able to absorb and assimilate the energies.

Aspire to be in the category of those who go still.

Here is one more important observation. There are some natural symptoms of progress in meditation such as:

- feeling of an upward pull from the *mūlādhāra cakra* (natural *mūla-bandha*) and *svādhiṣṭhāna cakra*,
- natural *aśvinī-mudrā*,
- feeling of an inward pull of the navel region (natural *uḍḍiyāna bandha*),
- quasi-electric sensation on the energy channels,
- feeling of pressure from within in the regions of the *cakras*, especially at the *ājñā cakra*, forehead or even the skull.

These are welcome marks of progress as explained in *Philosophy of Hatha Yoga*.

However, some neurological imbalances can also produce *kuṇḍalinī*-like symptoms. So, one may need to consult a neurologist in such cases.

What to do in response to the stirrings caused by the in-pouring of energies? Here are some answers.

It is not necessarily a high spiritual state. One is in the presence of a power but one's own vessel is weak. This vessel is unable to contain, absorb, assimilate the force being poured, so the force is being wasted in the form of a kinetic motion.

A spiritually advanced person would simply contain, absorb, assimilate the force whereby his/her own energies will be enhanced; his/her concentration will lead others to feel concentrated, centred, stilled, in his/her presence or through his/her spoken guidance; then one is a teacher.

In any case, many people do not maintain the correct posture when receiving such *prasādam*. A correct spine, and relaxed neuro-musculature are the first steps in absorbing and assimilating such energies instead of wasting them kinetically in some kind of a dramatic-looking motion.

Quite often, such experiences are momentary only. They last for the duration of one's staying in the sacred presence and then vanish. In such cases,

- just pay a mental homage, and
- remember the presence that was gracefully granted, and
- continue the self-purification and meditation practices as before.

If the movement persists, seek to absorb it by relaxation, stillness practices and breath awareness.[3]

It should be borne in mind, as we have said, that quite often disturbed neurological conditions mimic *kuṇḍalinī* experiences. In many cases it is advisable to consult a neurologist to make sure that there is no neurological disorder taking place in the body.

---

[3] See this author's booklet *Breath Awareness Practices in Different Traditions,* ahymsinpublishers@gmail.com

If there is no neurological disorder present and the movement persists, seek the help and guidance of one who has attained a degree of stillness in *kuṇḍalinī*. Such a one knows the subtle art of using his/her internal energy flows to channellize yours. S/he will catch you in the field of the stillness of her/his dynamic and well-channelized net of energies, will guide your breath and the energy field and will lead you into stillness.

She may guide you through appropriate practices such as visualizing the breath flowing through the spine or concentration in *kūrma nāḍī*,[4] and so on. Many of these *kriyā*s require initiation into special *mantra*s to go along with these practices.

There is, however, no substitute for personal meditation, *japa*, self-purification and similar pillars of *sādhanā*, spiritual endeavour.

---

[4] An energy channel curled up like a turtle in the lower chest; see *Yoga-Sūtra*s 3.31.

5

Honey of the Gods – 1

KUṆḌALINĪ is a term one hears often in spiritual circles, reads about and has dramatic expectations of; one hopes somewhere to touch some really live electric current and receive a cosmic shock.

No doubt that there are beings who are walking power stations, but they are masters and the first mastery is the mastery of the art of withholding and restraining. In the training of a soldier, teaching someone to shoot is the simplest part of the training; withholding the shot until the order is given is the most difficult part. The first is a crash, the second is a discipline, and *yoga* is a discipline. The definition of discipline is "that which a disciple goes through".

The words *kuṇḍalinī* and "consciousness" are more or less synonymous. In the Yoga philosophy, consciousness is not something that is object related. Ours is a philosophy of consciousness without an object. We encounter many who have known nothing but dead objects — be it a piece of cloth, gold, diamonds or the physical body — they do not recognize the riches that consciousness, pure consciousness, holds, or is. So they often speak of the *kuṇḍalinī* in us. We read vague references to this power and, adventurous explorers that we are, we want to climb the mountain; we want to climb the mountain where there is the cave in which she dwells.

Because the human language is so inadequate for things formless, we are unable to give this force any kind of a satisfactory description or definition, or even to assign a gender. The problem is that we have suffered and are suffering from aeons long amnesia, of 1,000 incarnations duration, an identity crisis in which we have forgotten our nature, our very being. Whatever colour clothing somebody puts on us, we say, "I am that colour; I am the colour".

There is an old story of a great sage who sat in meditation — in unbroken meditation — for 1,000 years, till the ants built nests around his body. All the forces that ascended through him were so powerful that the vibration reached through him all the way up to the throne of the King of Paradise, Indra.

Now, the residents of Paradise are always scared of someone doing a great deal of *tapas* (ascesis) because the power is such that it might topple the throne of heaven. In the hope of preventing that happening they always send tempters and temptresses down. So they did. But nothing happened to the great sage; his eyes remained closed in deep meditation.

The power coursing through him, bursting through the solar gate, kept shaking the throne of the King of Paradise, who got quite worried and came down himself. Pushing through the ants' nest and removing it, he addressed the great sage, "Sir, why do you continue to sit here in meditation? Now come with us, you are fit to dwell in paradise. You have earned the privilege!"

Now, that *ṛṣi* was not interested in any paradise; he was only interested in liberation. Paradise is also a very confined space. It may stretch for uncounted billion galaxies, but compared to infinity it is as confining as this body. Imagine staying in the same room (the body) for eighty years never taking a walk! Some people feel so secure staying inside the room, that they have no desire to go out. But those who have taken a walk outside the body say, "come on, it's very beautiful outside; there's brilliant light there".

So, the *ṛṣi* wasn't going to subject himself from one claustrophobia (of being in a little body) to another claustrophobia (of being in a paradise that extends only to a few billion galaxies); he wasn't interested in a myriad-galaxy long span over which the King of Paradise, Indra, ruled.

Nothing short of infinity would do for him.

*Yogī*s are ambitious people.

But the King of Paradise insisted, "come".

The *yogī* asked, "What is there in your paradise?"

Indra replied, "Well, we are adorned by a kind of gold that is not found on this earth; and we have fragrances before whom a million lotuses in all the ponds of this earth are faint. The beauty of celestial singers and dancers, the celestial maidens called *apsaras*es is unsurpassed. Come with me. I will arrange to show you the dance of the chief *apsaras,*[1] celestial dancing woman. Have you ever seen a woman?"

---

[1] *Apsarases* are the race of female singers and dancers of the celestial region. It is from the word *apsaras* that the Iranians got the word *parī*, which then became the word "fairy". In *A Midsummer Night's Dream* Shakespeare speaks of the fairies' →

The *ṛṣi* replied, "no".

Indra forcefully refreshed the invitation to him, "Do come with me".

So the great *yogī*'s curiosity was aroused and he went along and was seated on a throne almost as rich as Indra's own. The chief *apsaras* of the celestial court presented the dance of the seven veils. (Only a practising *yogī* can understand what the seven veils are, and what the dance of the seven veils means.)

She came in wearing a yellow veil and the *yogī* thought, "Oh! A woman is yellow", never having seen one before. He said, "I did not know a woman was yellow".

Indra said, "no, no, no, no, no. You just wait".

The *apsaras* danced and danced and she removed the yellow veil and out came a white one.

"Oh! She's white!"

Indra said, "No, *yogī*. You have been sitting too long with your eyes closed; you know nothing!"

"Oh, she's not white?"

Indra said, "no, no! that's just another veil".

So she danced as she had never danced before, because she was charged with the task of protecting her king's throne from the power of the great sage who could not be allowed to accumulate any more power. Somehow, if such power could be reduced, King Indra's throne would be safe.

→ homeland being in India, and the boy over whom Queen Titania was fighting with her husband, had been picked up by the fairies from a cave in India. In reading *A Midsummer Night's Dream* one finds many references to *yoga* symbolism.

So first, there was a yellow veil, and then a white veil; thus the yellow, white, red, grey, blue, crystal colour and then the seventh, which is not really a veil.

Thus she danced, and she dropped each veil one after the other. She dropped all the veils, and only the body remained. The *yogī* was getting very impatient as the dance went on for a long time.

He said, "And when will she drop that veil?"

"That final veil she cannot drop", he was told.

The *yogī* came away very disappointed, for, the body-veil had not been dropped so he could see "woman".

When all these veils are dropped, the woman who remains is *kuṇḍalinī*. So, the *yogī* went back into *samādhi* to dwell with the woman without the veils, the *kuṇḍalinī* force.

- When there are no more accoutrements,
- no more qualifications to your consciousness,
- no more conditions to your consciousness,
- no more limitations on your life force of size, name, age or gender,
- when the life force dwells by itself within the Self,
- that is called the *kuṇḍalinī*.
- Then all limitations drop.

At present, the world in which you are living, the things you identify with, the conditions that you claim as your own, qualifications that you continue to gather, anything you can name is a limitation.

Anything that you own, that you have, that you experience, that you long to experience, that you contain is a limitation. It is a finitude.

What are the children of Mother Infinity doing playing with pebbles of finitude?

Granted the pebbles are colourful, but a pebble is colourful only so long as you have not seen a diamond. What is this, going out selling your rubies for the price of glass beads?

As a great saint said, "Imagine an expense of 21,600 a day without any income". This is our condition.

A human being is said to take 21,600 breaths in twenty-four hours. This is our expenditure. Where is the income? We use it up; the body withers, dries out and lies dead like a log.

So what the *yogī* was saying is that we should start earning something now and spend a little less. We should spend a little more slowly; and not spend it so fast.

The income comes from the *prāṇa* vibrations. This system of the veil of the mind and the veil of *prāṇa* over *kuṇḍalinī* has to be understood.

Prāṇa mind and *kuṇḍalinī* are three distinct but interwoven forces. The word "forces" is used with great care. When the *kuṇḍalinī*, which is the unconditioned, unqualified life force, imparts a semblance of its aliveness to the body and infuses in it something that thrills it, makes it mobile, that little drop of *kuṇḍalinī*'s aliveness gives this body a semblance of aliveness that is called *prāṇa*.

When *kuṇḍalinī*, the unqualified, unconditioned consciousness imparts to this personality a semblance of awareness, then that drop of the force is called the "mind". Without this, the body is a log with a hollow pumpkin, a head, on top with a few holes in it, and a candle burning inside.

Prāṇa does not flow directly; it flows through the mind. Hence, without mastering the veil of *prāṇa* we do not go to the mind, and without penetrating through all the layers of the mind we do not go to the *kuṇḍalinī*. That is a long journey.

Prāṇa and the mind are also attracted by exterior forces, but their primary substrate, the essential bedrock of their existence is derived from this unconditioned life force. If your will is strong enough, you can break through the veils in just the flick of a finger. You see, infinity does not mean adding a trillion years to a trillion years to a trillion years and multiplying the sum of those three trillion years with another three times trillion years, thinking we will get to infinity. That is not the way to reach infinity. If we count all the particles of dust on this earth as the ants of the world seem busy doing, would we learn the nature of the earth? It's hard to understand the earth as a *whole*, and not count the dust particles, but people think that infinity comes when we have counted all the numbers.

There's a short cut to infinity, and that is like the flick of a finger, because in every moment there is infinity. Every moment arises out of infinity and merges back into infinity. Every subatomic particle arises out of a substratum of energy and merges into that substratum of energy. It is not that one moment leads to the next moment; the moment arises out of infinity, merges into infinity, then the next moment arises spontaneously. So the gateway to infinity is between two micro-moments. If we have a razor sharp enough to use as a wedge between moments, we can take a plunge through that wedge and bathe in infinity. For that, the mind has to be refined enough to catch what, for the want of a better word, may be called "the space between two micro-moments". We can really refine and further refine our awareness and use that awareness to cut through the space between two micro-moments.

We cannot go deep within by resorting to objects; they are too thick and blunt. We need something sharp like a vibration. We need to let our minds ride the vibration, and then enter.

There is a term in the Tantra texts called *prāṇa kuṇḍalinī*. Because we have *prāṇa,* the totality of our vital force field follows the same path that *kuṇḍalinī* follows. The first step is the awakening of the *prāṇa* field. The *prāṇa* field is the glue between the cell and the cell. The mystery of life itself is not in chemistry; that is a miracle so far as physical sciences are concerned. We can explain the how of that operation, but we cannot explain the *why* of the operation through the physical sciences. It is possible for two individuals with physical conditions that are exactly alike to be placed in an equally infectious environment and for one to become infected and for the other one not so; and that is because of their state of *prāṇa*.

The intensity of the aliveness of *prāṇa* depends on the healthiness of the mind, which is another force. In spite of all the advances made in psychology and all the talk of unconscious mind and the role that it plays in our lives, we human beings still suffer from a great curse. It is like somebody cursing us: "You shall become a statue, but stay alive and stay aware." We don't know it, but that is the fate that has befallen us.

The statue has been granted a little freedom of movement, but nothing like a force field. Having been cursed with becoming a statue, we relate only to the visible and the tangible — that which can be seen with the eyes, that which can be heard with the ears, that can be touched with the fingertips.

Consequently, we are unable to cross the boundary from the finitude of physically tangible artefacts and objects into that which leads to freedom.

Freedom here does not mean choosing among many finitudes, because that is bondage, going from one finitude to another finitude, exchanging one prison cell for another prison cell. It appears that we all have the freedom to move about so long as we don't step out of the prison walls of finitude. But that is no freedom.

Freedom is the ability to choose infinitude. When we realize that freedom, then we are free and the gate out of this prison is wide open!

But we are like a blind man who was confined to a room and was told that there is a door out. He decided to walk around touching the walls. Now, at a certain point he felt an itch, so he scratched the itch and kept walking. He walked all around the room but never found the door out, because each time he arrived near the door this itch got him and he had to scratch.

So we all have the freedom to rise from everything that limits us and makes us finite, and yet, when we come to the door we have these itches and we pass by the door. But the door is wide open.

Everyone who has ever practised any physical *yoga* knows there's a very strange thing about *yoga* practices: with other exercises one is tired after an exercise session but with *yoga* practice, one may be tired before but after doing the *yoga* practice the tiredness has vanished. The secret is that the *yoga* is not a set of physical exercises; they are *prāṇa* exercises. When we are tired, our *prāṇa* is bound, as it were; the field is divided up, and it's not flowing freely.

In *yoga* practices, we bring our awareness to the wholeness of the body, to the flow of the breath; that awareness is the mind's condition. The mind, therefore, being subtler than the *prāṇa* force, is able to break the barriers that have developed in the *prāṇa* field. The subtler is always more powerful than something relatively coarse.

If one goes through the exercises mindlessly one does not awaken *prāṇa*. So, the first step to awakening the *prāṇa* is doing the physical *yoga* exercises with *awareness*; without the awareness it is ordinary exercise, it is not *yoga*; it is a circus act. Anybody can touch his nose to his knees. The difference between the art of a contortionist and the art of an expert in *yoga* postures is that in *yoga*, gradually one begins to become aware of the centres of *prāṇa* and then learns to work directly on the *prāṇa śakti*, on the *prāṇa* force.

People like to take a course about *prāṇa*, but first it is important to describe what it is that you experience when your *prāṇa* is awakened. These are matters of experience, not of description and definition.

One can write a million pages on the nature of sleep and be so busy writing that s/he can't sleep any more, but a volume on sleep is not going to help an insomniac, unless he falls asleep out of boredom reading it! If you have experienced sleeping, can you describe it to someone who has never slept? You may be able to define all the body chemistry. You can say what hormone the pituitary or the pineal gland is secreting to induce sleep. You can speak of the rapid eye movement in a certain phase of sleep. You can provide measurements and graphs. You can even put them in a computer nowadays. You could hook the person to the computer but he's still not going to experience sleep.

What happens internally to a human being is a matter of experience alone. If someone has never suffered pain, all the descriptions of the chemistry of pain are useless to him because pain is an internal experience. If someone has never fallen in love, he can read all the poetry in the world and do a perfect literary analysis and criticism; he can tell the reason for the poet's choosing this form of diction and that metre, but love means nothing to him beyond a vague longing to know.

Everything that happens inside a human being is primarily a non-verbal experience. It is a mode of consciousness. It is something happening to the field called the life force. No matter how much the knowledge of chemistry is refined, it cannot impart the experience and it cannot really explain the experience that one has had. That is why the masters always emphasize experience; until we seek experience, all of this kind of writing is sāttvic entertainment. Sāttvic entertainment, however, is better than all the rājasic and tāmasic ones.

Do aspire for more than entertainment; aspire for a spiritual experience. Every experience we have is a *kuṇḍalinī* experience. This is what the Tantras say: without this life force there is no experience. This force is flowing continuously, and is dynamically vibrant. What happens when you touch something like an apple? The apple does nothing. An expert in neurology and brain chemistry will give us his own explanation, and we have no quarrel with that as far as the findings of modern science go, explaining all the chemical messages that go on in the neurons and the synapses. But only by first hand experience, by having touched things, do we know about touching.

The unified force field of consciousness needs a juxtaposition and thereby knows itself. You are this one unified force field. A child is born male or female. That newborn child couldn't care less whether it was a male or a female. Others give it this name: "You are a male. You are a female. We'll call you Sarah. We'll call you Sam". Only when the male meets the juxtaposition of the female does he know himself to be a male. In a planet full of males, nobody would know they are males. The female meets the male, and through that juxtaposition knows herself to be female. But if there were only females, nobody would know they are females. This is the nature of finitude.

Finitude means factoring the opposites; it means duality; it means a juxtaposition; it means a relationship. Anything which comes in the confines of finitude cannot survive, cannot continue, without that juxtaposition, without a relationship; it gets lonely and restless: Something is missing. We may think that maybe it is a larger bank account or better clothes, or a Concorde airplane. These are all examples of consciousness looking for a juxtaposition to assert its own self-knowledge.

This force field, this dynamic force field, is ever active. It is active in our eyes; through the juxtaposition of music it knows itself to be flowing in the ear. The *yogī* is one who needs no juxtaposition; who knows self to be self, by self, within self in his totality, and not limited to one sense experience and another. He does not need an apple in his hand to know that the fingers touch, because he simply experiences the field; because he is the field. We are the force field of life, of consciousness; and this force field is also the force field of *kuṇḍalinī*. So, whatever we experience, we experience nothing but *kuṇḍalinī*.

The only difference is that when a *yogī* experiences something by way of juxtaposition, he asks himself where the experience is coming from. The apple did not invite him to touch it. The diamond did not jump out of the jeweller's showcase and ask to be looked at. No doubt, some rays emanating from the diamond did touch the cornea of his eye. So the *yogī* traces it from eye to the core, to the very centre of the life force, from which, like the corona spreading out hundred million miles from the sun, all of our energies, all of our sensations, all of our perceptions are radiating out, bathing the world with the light of consciousness.

If we had the choice, would we rather be *in* the core, or be the core of the sun, or would we rather be the little corner of a cave on earth into which a tiny trickle of light fell accidentally? We identify with the diamond, but the *yogī* identifies with the core of the sun; he knows himself to be that. He talks about it to raise your aspirations; he tries to raise your aspiration in every different way — by story, by song, by simple example, by healing touch, by love, by smiles, by publications, by establishing institutes.

The great Śaṅkara, writing his commentary on the *Brahma-Sūtras* says: "Oh, somehow, may this worldly pain cease for these beings." Motivated by this compassion the *yogī* works ceaselessly to reduce and eliminate the beings' pain through his teaching of meditation.

A force field has its own dynamics, its own pathways. By self-awareness and consciousness we will learn of those pathways. All it takes is awareness, nothing else; there is no technique. All techniques are summed up in one word: awareness.

Deepen your awareness of yourself, and make it a *unitary* awareness; not awareness through the eyes, not awareness through the ears, not an awareness of this object or that object, this perception or that sensation, but the totality of awareness.

We come alive after our *yoga* practice because there is a totality of awareness of the entire body; the mind and *prāṇa* flow through the body. The exercises that teachers teach, and even the ones they are not yet allowed to teach, will come to us naturally when the *kuṇḍalinī* awakens. You'll only have to check out with the teacher, "Is it correct? This that is happening to me?" — and then you do nothing thereafter.

Then there is the cosmic *kuṇḍalinī*. We are all vortices in an ocean of light. Within the vortices there are smaller vortices and within those vortices there are yet smaller vortices. Not knowing our nature as vortices of energy within vortices, within vortices within larger vortices of life force and consciousness force, we think and utter idiocies. The energies that pass between the vortices, among the vortices, we do not see. But the *yogī* draws from the cosmic *prāṇa*, because he is one with the largest vortex of energy.

The only technique for waking to it is awareness; keep deepening your awareness of yourself. Make it as unitary as you can; the awareness of the total body. Be aware of what is happening in the totality — and eliminate qualifying and quantified conditions. Eliminate qualifying conditions such as "this one here", "that one there", "the hand versus the foot", "the digestive vortex as against the thinking vortex". These vortices are called *cakra*s. The whole universe consists of *cakra*s.

Centre on anything, but go deep: ask yourself "From where does this arise within me?", "By what force am I made alive?", "I said 'I'; who said that?" Go to the very root of that thought; observe the arising of the thought "I". Soon the word "I" will vanish, and only the awareness of being will remain. From where does this awareness of being come in me?

One day you will sit with your eyes open, looking into yourself, the eyes will close by themselves, and you'll have the awareness of the totality of this dynamic field. Do not go for those experiences out there; go for the experiencer. Look for the experience. Find out who wanted the diamond. Define the "me". Was it your eye? The eyes saw the diamond; was it the eyes that wanted the diamond? Who wanted the diamond? Look for that one. And in that One, I assure you, is the light of all the diamonds of the world.

6

Honey of the Gods – 2

EARLIER, we have described human beings as resembling individual "energy packs" or cells.

The Upaniṣads tell us: "That sun is the honey of God" and the universe is a honeycomb. The universe is a honeycomb with many cells, each filled with honey. The cells are divided, but the honey is not — the honey pours and flows. The cells are many, but the honey is one. Hexagon upon hexagon of the honeycomb — uncountable cells in the entire universe, all filled with honey. This is a very sweet universe.

Wherever I travel, I find that sweetness; there is no Chinese sweetness or Japanese sweetness, no separate American, Hindu, Muslim, or Jewish sweetness. Each of these cells contains the same honey. People everywhere are so reluctant to hurt others that when I find any bitterness in someone's mind it surprises me, and I wonder from where such an anomaly originates.

The universe is filled with the honey of God. This body — the universe — is a honeycomb. When people think of the universe, the immediate picture in their minds is, "I am here, and the universe is out there". We do not realize that the universe and everything that can be stated about the universe also includes us. It is like a single hexagonal cell in the honeycomb saying of that honeycomb, "This is me and over there is the honeycomb", as though that single hexagonal cell has nothing to do with the honeycomb as a whole. But the honey that is in this cell is also the honey in the rest of the comb.

Our bodies and our personalities are also honeycombs. The universe is composed of thousands of cells upon cells, and the honey of the life force flows through the honeycomb, through each of us. In each of us this honey is gathered from the flower garden of *śakti*, so it may flow through the entire honeycomb of our person.

Every time we meditate, we take a walk in the flower garden. It is composed of the lilies, the lotuses, and the roses of the *cakra*s — our flower garden. Otherwise, why is it that everyone in the world loves flowers?

For everything that we love in the universe, there is something within us that loves it because it sees its own image therein. In all the flowers of the world we see the image of our energy fields, which are centred so that the energy flows out like the petals of a flower opening, and returns like the petals of that flower closing.

In the Western world, these flowers are called roses because lotuses do not grow in the colder climates of Europe. So the original symbolism shifted to roses, such as "The Rose of the Heart", "Rose of the Cross", and "Rose of the Christ's wound". This is a trans-cultural shift, but the essence is the same.

Why did the *yogī*s choose the symbolism of the lotuses to describe the *cakra*s? This is because the lotus flower is unique — it opens at the touch of the morning sun and closes in the evening. Where is the sun whose touch opens our lotuses, and by whose withdrawing of the light do our inner lotuses close, so that we lose the awareness of our own eternally exuded fragrance? That sun is the same as the thousand-petal lotus, the lotus of all the lotuses. It is also called the thousand-rayed sun.

In the Yoga tradition one of the two highest sciences is called the solar science. Those who are initiated into the solar science no longer meditate; they are already awake, so they do not need to wake up. They no longer have to go into meditation because they never came out. If somebody is sitting comfortably in his house and you say to him, "When are you going home?" he would say: What are you talking about? Have you gone crazy? I'm at home! Those who are initiated into the solar science never "go into" meditation.

There is an ancient passage in Sanskrit that says,

> That you have to enter into meditation is the proof of your bondage and ignorance.

How do you still that which is already still? How do you illuminate that which is self-luminous? Do you pour perfume on jasmine to make it fragrant? Do you raise a candle so that with the light of that candle you may see the sun? With what eyes can you see your own eyes? With what other ocean are you going to fill the ever full ocean? What sugar could you sprinkle on a honeycomb filled with honey to further sweeten it? Follow the philosophy of fullness, and when you are aware of your own fullness, you feel that there is nothing wanting, nothing missing and you are ever joyful.

Joyful does not mean full of joy. It means the joy of fullness; joy that is fullness. The one who is aware of infinite fullness is aware of infinite joy. This is not a condition produced from outside. A silk or paper flower needs a perfume to make it fragrant. Many people think that meditation is something like sprinkling perfume on our lotuses, as though we have no natural perfume of our own. The essence of our being, the honey of these flowers, is distributed by the buzzing bees of *nāda* (internal sound) throughout every cell of this honeycomb called the body, the universe.

You crave honey because you have a salty taste in your mouth and bitterness in your heart, but the honeycomb is right here: it is in your fullness. If you see that somebody's honeycomb is empty, then fill it; there is plenty in you. If you have a full cup and someone else's cup is empty, why does that make you bitter, when your cup is full? If you are a loving, gentle person, fill that cup. Whatever you have, pour that out; live in the awareness of this fullness.

When you approach a honeycomb, from which part of the honeycomb should you sample to enjoy the sweetest taste? Some people, filled with anger, bitterness and the frustration of life, are led to the honeycomb and cannot sip from it, because they have so identified themselves with finitude that they have limited their capacity to enjoy their own fullness.

> Once there was a very thirsty man passing through an arid land; it was a long and arduous travel. He asked for the way to the river and another traveller said: Come along. I am going that way. It will be good company. We shall drink together from the river.
>
> The two walked together and came to the river. The guide bent down, cupped his hands and drank his fill.

> The other, who similarly had a parched throat due to the arduous journey, and who had been looking for a guide to show him the way, simply stood there with his mouth agape.
>
> The guide asked, "Hey, what's the matter? Why don't you drink?" The traveller replied, "There's too much water in the river to drink!"

This is the situation of people with limited capacity. Who is going to capture or imprison you if you do not drink the whole river? Take whatever you can; start wherever you want to. The honeycomb is all around you and inside you. Take honey from any cell that you want, you will still taste the same honey.

Wherever you are, start from there. You do not need to go anywhere else. When you are already home you do not need an aeroplane reservation to go home. Only when you are in exile do you need a ship, a boat, a vehicle, a horse carriage, an aeroplane, or a spaceship. You are sitting at home; there is no part of the infinite that is not the home of the infinite. From which end of infinity is your awareness going to migrate to some other end, so that your awareness may find itself?

There is nothing to this opening and closing of the eyes, being in meditation or being out of it, since the Infinity is everywhere — inside and outside. The arbitrary values and arbitrary boundaries of the inside and the outside are like putting an imaginary gate in the middle of the deepest part of the ocean. You may pass through the gate in the ocean where a sign points, "That way". But you may come this way also and if you pass through such a gate, you are still in the same ocean. There is no "in" and there is no "out". There is nothing to meditation; stop this entering and emerging and "going in" and "coming out". If you are already awake, you don't need to wake up. But if you're asleep, that's another matter. Unfortunately, we are all asleep and do need to wake into meditation.

The masters wander because their home stretches from infinity to infinity. They wander from room to room in their infinite home. Their house just happens to be larger than ours and covers many continents. So they wander, taking care of their home as you do, with a broom or a vacuum cleaner. Every now and then they grumble a little about the kids making the house dirty, "Every time I look, I have to clean up after you", but they keep cleaning the world up anyway. Every now and then one of the kids grows up and takes to discipleship and begins to help out.

There is a Tibetan story of a south Indian king, one of the eighty-four *mahā-siddha*s, great adepts, to whose court a great spiritual master came.

> A wandering master came to the court of this king and the king said, "Great master, you have such a hard life".
>
> He said, "Hard life? Whatever do you mean?"
>
> You wander from place to place, you have no home or fixed abode.
>
> The master replied: "It is you who have the hard life. You are a fixture in one place; you have no freedom. I have total freedom so I can wander where I please. You have to stay seated on a throne."
>
> The king said, "You are beginning to make sense. Tell me, how can I, a king who is bound to my duties, kingdom, country, subjects, and assigned role — how

can I remain true to it and also begin to enjoy the freedom that you have? Will you teach me the secret?

The master replied, "Yes, indeed. You are to go nowhere. Remain where you are; sit on your throne, do your duties, take care of your citizens, enjoy whatever there is to enjoy. I'll teach you one little technique, but outwardly you are to renounce nothing."

So the master taught him a *maṇḍala* (a meditational diagram) like a visual *mantra,* and told him to mentally draw that diagram on the tip of his right thumb, or, some versions say, to visualize it in the finger ring on his right hand. That's all he gave him to do.

Now, the thumb itself is a very important possession. In the Upaniṣads the Spiritual Self is called "thumb-sized", because all the body-hollows that mark the centres of consciousness can be measured externally by the thumb; you can put the thumb in the middle of the eyebrow, in the hollow of the throat, at the heart centre, and at the navel — the thumb tip fits at all those places.

So the master told the king: This is your spiritual practice. No matter where you are — sitting on the throne, dispensing justice to your subjects, in the company of your servants and maids — keep drawing this *maṇḍala* mentally on the tip of your right thumb. But it must remain a carefully guarded secret; a personal practice revealed to others loses half its potency.

Spiritual experience narrated to others loses its power. If people know that you meditate, half the effect of the concentration of meditation is dissipated. The true meditation is that which is held secret. Let no one know, and hold it like a treasure, close to your chest and heart.

If you want to teach others, you are to teach nothing. The honey will overflow; you do not need to argue about the qualities of honey with anybody. If you have honey and your honeycomb is full, it will overflow and sweeten others around you, but you are to say nothing. Understand this secret of successful, full, happy, joyous, and fulfilled teaching life and the life in general — secret meditation.

The secret of meditation is secret meditation. The secret of successful meditation is secret meditation, for which you seek no recognition, no honour and no respect. Instead, seek insult and you will succeed. It is said in the ancient *Lawbook of Manu*,

> A child of God should feel terribly agitated when faced with respect and honour, as though a poison cup is being presented to him.
>
> A child of God should seek out dishonour, as though he was being presented a cup full of the elixir of immortality.

So the king was advised to keep his practice secret and to guard this secrecy.

> As advised by the master, the king surrounded himself with all the possible luxuries — even the pillows in his bedroom softer than he had before! Much song and dance and revelry went on in his palace. There were beautiful maidens, great treasures, silk and velvet tapestries. He became a playboy king in the eyes of his subjects. Lila-pada was his name, or Lilapa, a hedonist *yogī*!
>
> Though he continued to have armies and to dispense justice, and was surrounded by all this revelry, song, dance, and beautiful maidens, he never let his mind

shift from the tip of his right thumb, on which he constantly mentally drew his *maṇḍala*.

During his whole life, no one suspected him of being in meditation. It was only by the manner of his death that he was recognized as a master, and was called Lila-pada,[1,2] the Venerable Player.

People ask teachers what their centre of consciousness is and on what *cakra* they should meditate. They think that someone will come with a key and open a *cakra*, just like that. But there is honey anywhere in the honeycomb. Every experience is a *kuṇḍalinī* experience. The problem is that you look for the object of the experience and get stuck in the limitations of the experience and do not look within for the Experiencer.

The objects of experience are there to provide a juxtaposition, a background against which you may know yourself. So long as you treat the objects of the universe and your sensory experiences as juxtaposition, they become triggers for your internal life. The honey flows inward and suffuses you even more.

This is so with any experience you have: for example, the experience of touching the back of your hand with your finger. Reverse the flow of sensation and see where the experience of touch originates. What flows from within you to the surface

---

1 The Sanskrit word *pada* meaning "foot" or "feet". It may be added to a name or to an epithet as an expression of reverence. The names of all 84 *mahā-siddhas* (great adepts) honoured in the Tibetan tradition end with the word *pada*, shortened to *pa*.

2 About the death of a master, read Swami Rama's *Sacred Journey* and this author's *Meditation and the Art of Dying*. Both are available from ahymsinpublishers@gmail.com

of the fingertip to become tactile sensation? Trace the path to its very source and you are in *kuṇḍalinī*. What part of the surface of your skin has this power? The same part as the part of the honeycomb you touch to start drinking honey — all of it. Any cell of the honeycomb, any cell of your person is the honey of the gods (*deva-madhu*). This is a very simple art.

Let us look at it another way: imagine that you have travelled from wherever you are to New York; you've got a map. When you get to New York and want to return, which road should you take? The road you've already taken to New York is the very same road you would take to come back, because you've already experienced it.

The road, the pathway, the channels of energy, through which your consciousness, energy, *prāṇa*, and mind have travelled, are called *mano-vaha nāḍī*s (the mind-bearing channels). These are the same channels you have taken to come out to the surface of the body from your inner core. You already had the map of those, or else how could you have come to the surface of your eye from the seat of your consciousness? You have a map that you followed.

From the deepest seat of your consciousness how did you manage to come to that part of your nostril that smells? From the seat of your consciousness how did you manage to create your taste buds? From the seat of your consciousness how did you happen to come to the conch-like cochlea, so that you could hear? Which road did you happen to take from the seat of your consciousness, your throne room, to the outside walls of the palace that you call the skin? Take the same road back.

You are like a king standing outside his palace asking the guards, citizens, and passersby, "Excuse me, do you mind telling me how I get to my throne room?", making yourself a laughing stock. People would say, "King, go back in the same way that you came out." That is the way to the seat of consciousness — even an infant knows the pathway. Adults often don't — that's the problem.

When an infant first opens its eyes to the world, by what process does this inner being know that eyes are for seeing? Light falls on the retina and reminds us. How does an infant know what nerves to use for speaking? He has never seen anybody speak; he has heard people's sounds, but he has never actually witnessed the process of speaking, and still he re-learns the pathway. As you would explore a city, an infant explores his body and learns the pathway by which a thought that is in the mind may be brought to his tongue as a word, following the appropriate *mano-vaha nāḍī*s.

If you seek to discover how to re-enter into silence, you follow the same pathway back — the one you discovered as an infant and used for speaking. Do you really think that you don't know the pathway back as a grown up adult, when you were able to find the same as an infant? There are paths going to the centre of the city of consciousness through all the gates of the fortress — paths from the eyes and ears and all of the senses going to the centre of the city. There are also paths through all the active senses — the hands with their ability to receive and give, the organ of elimination, the organs of generation and pleasure, through the navel, the heart, the throat and through the centre between the eyebrows. They are all *cakra*s; vortices. Go into the centre of the vortex, go into the depth.

In the tāntric texts there are many lists of points of concentration: the fingertips, toe tips, ankles, knees, mouth, certain points in the pelvic organs and a bulb (*kanda*) in the perineal area, which is the seat of the *kuṇḍalinī*. When some of these sensations are dissipated outwards they become "sex" or other pleasures; the same sensations drawn inwards and upwards to their source become the awakening of *kuṇḍalinī*.

Similarly there are other points of concentrations of energy: the navel centre, the stomach, the heart centre, the *kūrma nāḍī* between the heart centre and the throat, the throat centre, the palate, the centre between the eyebrows, the centre of the forehead and the top of the head.

Then there is another term in the Tantras which means, "the end of twelve". If you check yourself, you will find a distance of roughly twelve finger widths each

- from the genital centre to the navel centre,
- from the navel centre to the heart centre,
- from the heart centre to the throat centre,
- from the throat centre to the space where the nose bridge touches the upper lip — which is a continuation of the *ājñā* centre, and semi-finally
- a space of twelve finger widths from the *ājñā* centre between the eyebrows to the top of the head.

There's also a point of concentration twelve finger widths above the head. There's also a point of concentration twelve finger widths in front of the nostrils, which brings you back to the heart centre. This distance, twelve finger widths, is a term in Tantra called *dvādaśānta*.

True, in different people some channels are more open than others. You can easily find out about yours by examining your breathing process, and that is why we teach breath awareness. Your awareness of the breathing process replaces the random arousal of sentiments, emotions and moods. The awareness of your *mantra*, which is the inner buzzing bee that gathers honey from the flowers, replaces the arousal of random thoughts.

There are honey-bees in us and there are wasps. The wasps also buzz, but they produce no honey. All kinds of tape recordings go on in the head. To get rid of these wasps, follow the honey-bees; they'll fetch honey for you. Your life can become so honey filled that the transient and miserably miserly pleasures of the world lose their value, when you realize how full is the fullness of that sun which is the honey of God.

Contemplate on these thoughts; keep continuously reminding yourself that this fullness and perfection is everywhere, like the playboy king, who constantly drew his mental *maṇḍala* on the tip of his right thumb and thus became a master. You can too; begin by remembering that you are the honey of the gods.

7

Eternal Swan

THE word for swan in the Vedas is *haṁsa*. This swan dwells in the sky of the inner vision and is the vehicle of the Virgin Mother of wisdom, Sarasvatī. She is the guest dwelling in this house of the body, but she is born of the eternal law and the eternal truth.

In India, string instruments like the *sitār* or the *vīṇā* are often shaped like a swan; their strings represent the lines of *kuṇḍalinī* in the subtle body from where all music, all manifestation, arises. The goddess of wisdom and music, Sarasvatī, is often depicted carrying the multi-stringed *vīṇā*, on which the *mantra*s of the Vedas are sung.

Eternal truth, the river of *kuṇḍalinī*, originates in the high mountains at the crown of the head. Born of the speech of divine inspiration, *kuṇḍalinī* descends, to dwell in the most sacred places within us. Sarasvatī is also the ancient word for *kuṇḍalinī*. Sarasvatī also means river, while *saras* means pool. *Kuṇḍalinī* flows from her source to create seven major pools — seven *cakra*s around which the subtle body is established. The incoming and outgoing breaths are the wings of this eternal swan, the one on which Sarasvatī flies.

Kuṇḍalinī contains all divine light and divine sound, from which the entire physical universe comes into existence. In a human being, two forces arise from *kuṇḍalinī* to create the personality. These are *manas* (mind) and *prāṇa* (vitality). These two manifest in the physical body, but their material aspects receive life from infusion of the light of consciousness and vigour that flows from *kuṇḍalinī*. You have the ability to function only because that infusion of power, that thrill of energy — of superconsciousness — constantly moves up and down your spine.

You are not apart from *kuṇḍalinī*; you do not have *kuṇḍalinī*; you are *kuṇḍalinī*. In a living organism, pulses are sent out from the centre of awareness. These pulses become the two major aspects of our being — awareness and aliveness.

To run any kind of electrical device, you need parts and connections. Electricity can make the blades of a fan move only if there is a connection. When the fan is plugged into the wall, current passes through a wire and brings a pulsation to magnetic coils. Those coils alter the energy and produce a different kind of pulse, one that can move the fan blades and create motion.

Likewise, behind the movement of my hand is the power of *kuṇḍalinī*. Without that power, it would be a dead man's hand. This infusion of power from the superconsciousness that runs up and down the spine is not direct. It must first pass through certain stations where it is transformed into the requisite form of energy. A fan is run by electricity, but it cannot become a heater, a TV or a stereo set. For electricity to serve all of those functions, different intermediary mechanisms are required. *Kuṇḍalinī* also needs intermediary mechanisms to transform its power into the specific kind of energy necessary to operate one's personality. Those power stations in the path of this river of light are the seven *cakra*s.

Kuṇḍalinī is not distant. It is an integral part of what you are. It is evident in the symmetry of your body. Have you noticed how your body is divided by a fine hairline? Have you seen how, in the front and back, this hairline runs? These are demarcation lines of the *kuṇḍalinī* that resides in the subtle body.

In different spots, you may notice that the hairline forms little whorls. This is evidence of the *cakra*s. Everything in your body is marked in relation to *kuṇḍalinī*, just as iron filings indicate the lines of a magnetic field.

Your body was not created accidentally. Three thoughts unite in the moment of conception. Their power is such that the life, light, consciousness, awareness and luminosity are drawn to that place of union. The power of the union of the mother thought, the father thought and the thought of the child is such that a little spark is activated. That tiny speck of a living being, glued to the walls of the mother's uterus, already has an energy field, the spark of *kuṇḍalinī*. Along the lines of that energy field the body grows. Your body is built along the lines of this *kuṇḍalinī* field.

At the *maṇipūra cakra* (navel centre) some 72,000 *nāḍīs*, (energy channels) radiate out, creating the currents and cross-currents of the subtle body. But this river of light creates two major channels of energy, called *iḍā* and *piṅgalā*. These are the principal energy channels — left and right, respectively — in the subtle body that can be imagined as running from an area that roughly corresponds to the base of the spine in the physical body to the nostrils.

Immediately upon coming into being, the *kuṇḍalinī* force becomes polarized. This occurs because we are ignorant of our unity. But her true nature is one light, a potentially free-flowing singularity that can be made to flow in *suṣumṇā*, the central *nāḍī*. *Suṣumṇā* can be imagined as beginning at the base of the spine and terminating in the skull.

Iḍā and *piṅgalā*, the left stream and the right stream, are pictured as two snakes wrapped around a central pole. This is the caduceus. Naturally, these three channels have to interact; in the vicinity of those interactions, eddies and whorls are created. These are the *cakra*s. Although *kuṇḍalinī* differentiates itself at the various *cakra*s, it remains the same primal force.

Mother and child are linked at the navel centre, both physically and in the subtle body. The child draws both physical nourishment and *prāṇa* from its mother. It even draws contents from the mother's mind. Before birth, the child is receiving subtle content from the mother; the two minds are connected. When the child is born, a telepathic link between mother and child remains.

Every human being is born telepathic, but we forget. We bury ourselves in this clay pot, saying,

> This body is me and there is nothing else to me. There is nothing of the spirit in me; I am just a body. I got this life force by accident. I received these parents by chance. I didn't ask to be born!

There are more minute and subtle forces functioning in our personalities than we can imagine. The *yogī*s are in tune with these forces. They walk in awareness of them. They know how to link their energies with those of the disciple — to reach out and help a disciple's meditation and raise his or her *kuṇḍalinī* to a higher level of consciousness. This is the art of the masters.

Some people wonder if *kuṇḍalinī* is specific to human beings alone. Actually, *kuṇḍalinī* is the life force in all creatures. However, karmic limitations are superimposed on *kuṇḍalinī* which is why it does not develop into the full power of mind and *prāṇa* in sub-human species or even why it awakens in different degrees from person to person.

People also ask if the *cakra*s are in the back of the spine or in the front of the body. The answer is neither. The *cakra*s are not in the physical body. If I hold a magnet in my hand, is its magnetism in the top or the bottom? Is it at the front or the back? It's all around; it's a field and in that field there's no front or back. So it is with the *cakra*s — there is no front or back.

Because *kuṇḍalinī* performs different functions as it passes through each force field, the *cakra*s are sometimes referred to as psycho-physiological stations. But for a fully awakened person, the idea of seven *cakra*s has no real value. For an enlightened one, there is only one *cakra* — *sahasrāra* — whose vicinity is the crown of the head. Such a blessed one has complete access to the wellspring of consciousness and can enter the superconscious state whenever he or she wishes. In such a high state, the notion of different kinds of psychology or levels of consciousness becomes completely meaningless. Rather, that person naturally uses his or her life force skilfully, as the occasion arises, and after discharging his/her duty flies with the swans of Sarasvatī to the regions of beauty and bliss.

8

Initiation into the Sun-Swan

THE Indian mind, like many other cultures, has maintained an unbreakable and intimate relationship with Sūrya (sun) from times immemorial. Here we intentionally do not translate the word *sūrya* as the sun. This is because of the common human limitation that the mind becomes confined to associate certain words with certain forms and then refuses to budge into any level more expansive than the limitation imposed by such association. If the word *sūrya* were to be translated as the sun all its deeper spiritual meanings will be clouded and obscured. The inner meaning of the word *sūrya* will become clear only towards the end of one's spiritual pursuit.

The word Sūrya occurs in *R̥gveda* 421 times. Among many other names of Sūrya, the word *savitr̥* (birth-giver) occurs 174 times. In other words little over 15 per cent of the *R̥gveda* is dedicated to Sūrya. This does not include the hymns to Uṣas (dawn) who represents the spiritual sunrise. The most famous of the Sūrya hymns is the well-known Gāyatrī. The word means

> Guide and protector of *prāṇa*s,
> She who protects as she is sung.

She is also known as Sāvitrī she whose deity is Savitr̥. It was revealed to sage Viśvāmitra and occurs eight times in the major

Vedic Saṁhitās.[1] Like the rays of the sun, from Gāyatrī emanate numerous word-incarnations. For example, in the *Mahā-Nārāyaṇa Upaniṣad* we read nineteenth versions of Gāyatrī dedicated to various spiritual forces such as Rudra and Mahā-Lakṣmī. Commonly, twenty-four basic Gāyatrīs of various *iṣṭa devatās*[2] are recited, but there are many more. The daily prayer rituals (*nitya-karma*) must include fragrant water offerings (*arghya*) to Sūrya. The daily morning, afternoon and evening meditative prayer (*sandhyā*) is of course centred around Gāyatrī recitation.

Numerous texts extol Sūrya and explain his mysteries, for example, *Sūrya-Purāṇa*, *Sūrya-gītā*, and the Upaniṣads: *Haṁsa*, *Āruṇika*, *Mahā-Nārāyaṇa* and *Maṇḍala-brāhmaṇa*. Reading of these texts together with Vedic hymns will explain the meaning of *sūrya*. Only when we understand whom we worship can we comprehend the meaning of the form of worship.

Sūrya is also very closely associated with Viṣṇu or *Nārāyaṇa*, the Preserver Being in Cosmic Contemplation lying on the Serpent of the Residue on the Waters of Dissolution. In performing many ritual prayers we recite:

dhyeyaḥ sadā savitṛ-maṇḍala-madhya-vartī nārāyaṇaḥ

Nārāyaṇa is always to be meditated upon, dwelling in the centre of the orb of the sun.

The thousand names of Viṣṇu (Viṣṇu-sahasra-nāma) may also

---

[1] The texts as they have been recited mnemonically for thousands of years.

[2] Whichever form and name of the deity is one's favourite according to one's faith or choice. For further explanation, see *God*, by this author, available from ahymsinpublishers@gmail.com

be recited visualizing Sūrya and Viṣṇu as one. The advent of Viṣṇu in covering the whole universe in three steps (*Ṛgveda* I.22.20) has been explained by *ācārya*s to refer to the Sūrya's enactment of the power to remove darkness in three steps and points to the illuminations one receives in the earth–sky–heaven centres in the *cakra*s as one's consciousness ascends. *Sūrya* is often identified with *prāṇa* and resides in the *sūrya-nāḍī*, solar channel that is *suṣumṇā* (the central stream of the *kuṇḍalinī*). Being synonymous with *prāṇa*, *sūrya* is the healer of all diseases. In the worship to astrological deities (*nava-graha-pūjā*), the first honour is given to Sūrya with the *mantra*:

ā kṛṣṇena rajasā. . . . . (*ṚV* I.35.2)

The sage Śaunaka's text named *Ṛg-vidhāna* (I.93) states that one meditating on *sūrya* with this *mantra* will live a long life without illness. This not only has clear application in Ayurveda but also opens important dimensions in the practice of *yoga* such as *sūrya-namaskāra* which is performed with homage to twelve manifestations of the sun (Ādityas) with specific breath rhythms. Those who perform *sūrya-namaskāra* with breath rhythms and these *mantra*s twelve times daily are known to have lived to 100 years.[3]

Another aspect of the intimate spiritual relationship with *sūrya* is seen in the honours bestowed upon solar dynasties (*sūrya-vaṁśa*) like those of the royal dynasties of India and Japan. What does it mean to be of the solar dynasty? In the text dedicated to extolling the Acts of Divine

---

[3] Full knowledge of the twelve *mantras* of *sūrya-namaskāra*, together with six *bīja-mantras*, and their corresponding *āsana*s may be had from numerous publications on the topic and from any qualified *yoga* teacher.

Mother (*Devī-māhātmya*), King Suratha was granted the boon that he will be born from *sūrya* and will become Sāvarṇī, the next Manu.[4] What does it mean to be born from *sūrya*? Again, the next Buddha also is Maitreya, descendent of Mitra,[5] another name for *sūrya*. We cannot answer all the questions related to this in detail in a short chapter. But we can attempt to point to them briefly.

In *Gāyatrī-mantra*, the first word "That" (*tat*) is a key word of spiritual knowledge (*brahma-vidyā*). It is also seen in the Vedāntic great sentence (*mahā-vākya*) "That Thou Art" (*tat tvam asi*). Put together, the first word of *Gāyatrī* and the *mahā-vākya* signify: "That brilliance that we meditate upon is identical with 'That which thou art'". This interpretation is reinforced in the primary *mantra* by which *guru* (the remover of darkness) is worshipped in *guru-cakra*:

> *akhaṇḍa-maṇḍalākāram . . .*
>
> It is a laud to "He who has shown me *tat-padam*, that state which is expressed by the word that".

In *kuṇḍalinī-yoga*, which is the same as Śrī-vidyā, of the three *lokas*, seats of the levels of light, the second one is known as *sūrya-loka* (the solar world). An initiation *yoga-dīkṣa* in *sūrya-loka* prepares one to ascend to *candra-loka* (lunar world), the realm beyond *ājñā cakra* where the light no longer burns but cools. When *sūrya-nāḍī* bursts through

---

[4] In the cosmology of India, one cycle of creation is divided into fourteen *manvantaras*, each ruled by one Manu, the cosmic Sage who is the source of contemplative knowledge, *mantras* and powers of cosmic contemplation.

[5] Mitra was also worshipped by the ancient Iranians as a major Divine form, by the name Mithra. The same tradition then spread to the Roman empire where the deity became known as Mithras.

these *loka*s by the process of "piercing through the point" (*bindu-vedhana*) and makes the entire life force burst through thousand-arrayed *cakra* the *yogīn* becomes known as "one who has burst through the orb of the sun" (*sūrya-maṇḍala-bhedin*). Then, like Arjuna of the *Bhagavad-Gītā* (XI.12) one sees the light of thousand suns. So also in *Sūrya-gītā* sun's charioteer, Aruṇa, is taught the *brahma-vidyā* by *sūrya* with similar realizations. The entire process is explained in great detail in *Maṇḍala-brāhmaṇa Upaniṣad* and *Mahā-Nārāyaṇa Upaniṣad*; it is summarized in *Haṁsa Upaniṣad* where again, the supreme light as the supreme *haṁsa* shines with a splendour of ten million suns.

parama-haṁso bhānu-koṭi-prakāśaḥ . . .

The secret of *sūrya* within is contained in *haṁsa-mantra* which will be translated below. *Sūrya* in *haṁsa* form as the free-winged swan journeying through the skies of breath (*prāṇa*) and *sūrya-nāḍī* leads the *sādhaka* from the most external surfaces to the deepest interior. According to Śaunaka's *R̥g-vidhāna* (II.67) one who does *japa* of the *haṁsa-mantra* in his last moments goes to the eternal realm of *Brahman*. No wonder, Bhīṣma preparing to abandon his body is visited by *haṁsa*s; and in the very first verse of the King of Hymns (*stava-rāja*) (*Mahābhārata*, Śānti-parvan, 47.38) addreses Kr̥ṣṇa as "one whose self is the sun" (*sūryātman*).[6]

tasmai sūryātmane namaḥ

Prostrations to the Sun-Self.

These truths can be known experientially in the initiatory traditions only. The keepers of *sūrya-vijñāna* (solar science

[6] For details see this author's book, *Bhishma* (now to be published under a new title). ahymsinpublishers@gmail.com

branch of *yoga* of the highest order), who can impart a ray of the living and conscious sun to the disciple, are to be counted perhaps on the fingers of one hand. Those qualified to receive such knowledge may be even fewer. Those to whom such knowledge is granted are "born of the sun" and ascend to *mokṣa* (liberation) by the grace of the *guru*. Meanwhile the daily ritual offerings (*arghya*), *haṭha* practices like *sūrya-namaskāra* (solar salutation *āsanas*) and the *mantra-japa* with all its intricate steps in *sāvitrī-sādhanā* (*sādhanā* of *Gāyatrī*): these are initial preparations for those who aspire.

The Haṁsa-Mantra

haṁsah śuci-sad vasur antarikṣa-sad
hotā vedi-sad atithir duroṇa-sat ।
nṛ-sad vara-sad ṛta-sad vyoma-sad
ab-jā go-jā adri-jā ṛtam bṛhat ॥

(*Ṛgveda Saṁhitā* IV.40.5; *Vājasaneyiī* X.24; XII.14; *Taittirīya Saṁhitā* I.8.15.2; IV.2.1.5; *Taittirīya Āraṇyaka* X.10.2)

Haṁsa, the sun swan of *prāṇa*
dweller in purity
habitat of beings
entity that is all treasures
abiding in the spaces of inner vision
priest who pours oblations
sits in the fire altar
ever-wandering guest mendicant
sojourns in the house
dwells inside the humans
occupies the seat of boons
eternal truths his abode

entire space his place for meditation
born of the flow of waters
offspring of ever-inspired speech
child of the mountain
the great expansive
Brahmā-like universal law
and the very truth itself,
Haṁsa!

In brief, one declares in each breath *haṁso 'haṁso 'ham. . . .*

I am That: I am *haṁsa,* the sun-swan. *so 'ham,* I am that.

9

Knowing God*

ALWAYS remember that there is a difference between information and knowledge. You have read something, that is information. You are debating about it in the mind. That is also based on information. Most people think that that information is knowledge and they say to themselves "I have read so much, so I know". But that information is not knowledge. Knowledge is a personal experience.

That you have read about non-violence, that is not knowledge of non-violence. That you have experienced non-violence, practised it, that is the knowledge of non-violence. You have learned how to use non-violence in situations which will otherwise invoke violence. That is non-violence. You have read about advanced techniques of meditation, that is not knowledge. When you have the experience that those techniques give you, then even without the technique, you have knowledge. Your goal should be that knowledge.

You have read about God in many books, in many religions. That is not knowledge of God. You believe in God, that is not knowledge of God. That you know God personally, that is knowledge. So practice your meditation with that knowledge as your goal.

---

* Edited transcript of an address given to Korean initiates visiting Swami Rama Sadhaka Grama, Rishikesh.

When you have that knowledge, it shows itself in you. It shows itself in how you look. Do you have a loving look on your face? That a stranger looks at you and feels loved, a complete stranger looks at you and feels loved . . . that is the knowledge of God.

Your knowledge shows in the way you speak. Does your voice soothe others when you speak . . . then you have knowledge of God. Does it calm others when you speak, that is knowledge of God.

The way you move your body, inspires in others an appreciation for grace. That is the knowledge of God. Or knowledge of Christ, or knowledge of Buddha, or knowledge of Tao. All these phrases mean the same thing.

Many people who sit in meditation look for many experiences. The only experience that you need to look for is a state of calmness inside you. You have read that in meditation one will see lights and one will hear sounds. Forget about that. Does your body become calm and still? Does your heart become free of disturbed emotions? Does your breath slow down? How long does your mind remain calm and undisturbed even after you have opened your eyes from mediation? That shows whether you are meditating or not. That is knowledge of God.

When you see God not only in your friend, when you see God in your enemy and you act accordingly — that is the knowledge of God. When you enter a state of meditation, what you call meditation at this time, that initial stage will be left behind. You will go further. You will go deeper. You will become even calmer and greater illumination will come to you. Knowledge will start coming to you from within you.

You will read the same ancient texts that you have read in translation, but if you have been meditating, suddenly you will see a new meaning to their words. You will connect the meditation and the meaning to your experience.

If you have to make an effort to become calm, you are not meditating yet. If you have to make an effort to clear your mind, you are not meditating yet. When your mind remains in a state of calmness even when you are indulging in worldly activities, then it means that you have some experience of God.

At present God is only an imagination to you. It is only a belief system. You believe you have a diamond somewhere in your house. But you have never opened your shelves to check where that diamond is, what that diamond looks like. What is the value of that diamond to you? So at present you have a belief that there is a God, but you have not experienced Him what is the meaning of such a belief?

When your meditation progresses, certain changes occur in you. Your face changes: it becomes a calmer and more loving face. It becomes a more lovable face. Everybody looks at you and loves you in a very, very pure way. The way of your body changes. When you are sitting, people can feel a stillness in you. They're inspired by that stillness. By your stillness they become still. By that inspiration they become inspired. When you are moving, they feel a sense of beautiful grace about you — because then your movement is not jerky. There is patience in that movement. There is a flow in that movement. If your movement is jerky, then you have not yet begun to experience God.

When you have begun to experience God, when your meditation has begun to bear fruit, there are changes in your voice. Your voice becomes calm. Anyone who hears your voice becomes calm. A person comes to you very disturbed and by the way you say to him "hello", his mind calms down. Then you are on the path to God; you have begun to know God.

You argue about the nature of God, that is not loving God. That is loving words. That is loving your intellect that you are very proud of. That is a showing off of knowledge you think you have, but you don't have. One who has knowledge of God, does not try to define God, as to what God is like.

One who has knowledge of God listens to what others have to say about God. He agrees with whatever they say about God, because whatever they are saying is true to a certain extent. But it is not yet experiential truth. One who knows God agrees with everybody's opinion about truth.

One who knows God agrees with everybody's description and definition of God, however incomplete those descriptions and definitions might be. So if there is a question in your mind "Will I ever get to know God?", just see whether you show signs of knowing God. Whether you show signs of God-lovingness.

One who has come to know God remains in a state of silence, even when he or she is speaking. One who knows God remains in a state of fasting, even when he or she is eating or drinking — because the depth of his or her mind is not touched by that speech, is not touched by that eating and drinking. Such a mind is a God-loving mind, or a Christ-loving mind, or a Buddha-loving mind, or loving by whatever other name you want to give to your God.

One who knows God, forgets God's name. One who loves God, at first remembers God's name at all times. But when love reaches the place of knowing, then the nameless God shows Himself or Herself to you — because no words can reach God. No words can describe or define God. You ask such a God-knowing person about God. S/he sits dumb. That is the sign of a God-knowing person.

Inside you, outside you, around you, in front of you, behind you, below you, above you, is an ocean and you are like a piece of sponge in that ocean. That ocean is passing through the sponge and is all around that sponge. So the little sponge goes to the elder bigger sponge and asks: "Wise elder, where will I find the ocean?" What is the wise elder sponge going to reply?

He replies: The one passing through you, around you, below you, above you, on the sides of you, in front of you, behind you, and again passing through you, well, that is the ocean.

Please understand that you are like that sponge in the ocean of God.

So where will the sponge go to find the ocean? Will he take a pilgrimage from one end of the Pacific to the other end as there might be more ocean there and less ocean where he is? Is there less God in Korea and more God in Rishikesh? When you leave from a meditation teacher's lecture hall, will you leave the place of more God and go to the place of less God? Is that how it is?

Wherever you are, be in that ocean that is God. The person who begins to know God — some knowledge begins to flow through him, through her, without effort. There, love and knowledge are synonyms. Loving God and knowing God is one and the same thing. There can be no difference between the two.

So, let your idea of meditation be very clear. If you will use your meditation only like a boat, that you go a little distance with that boat and then abandon the boat in midstream, then you have not yet understood what your goals are. Remember that you are the river. You are this shore of the river, you are the opposite shore of the river, you are the flow, you are the waves. You are the boat, you are the pilgrim, you are the journey. These are names of one and the same being, that is you that is God that is you.

In meditation these words should not come to you. You should not be contemplating these words. It should become such for you, the river, this shore, the opposite shore, the flow, the pilgrim, the boat. All one and the same. I wish you that love of God, that knowledge of God.

Do not think that it is not possible for you to have it. Others received it. Why would you not? Carpenters doing carpentry have received it. Weavers weaving cloth have received it. Poets writing poetry have received it. Some laughing saints while laughing have received it. Some silent saints while in silence have received it. Celibate monks and nuns have received it. Married householders have received it. Robbers have received it, so have the thieves received it. Human history is full of names of these carpenters and weavers, laughing ones and silent ones, celibate ones and married ones, men and women, old ones and very young, child ones, robbers and thieves, who all received it. Why would you not receive it?

You will receive it.

I wish you that gift of Yourself to yourself, that gift of God to your God, in this very life. In this very life.

10

When I Left the Sun

"When I Left the Sun" is a prose poem. It is the story of the Hero's Cosmic Journey, the archetypal story of which all others are variants. It is the tale of a Ray of Light that has been ensnared in time and space, in the darkness of the material world, forgets his true nature, and longs for a Light that he can only vaguely recall. He suffers, weeps, prays, receives a little Luminosity from those Rays who are not ensnared, remembers his true nature, aspires for his true Homeland, and "gains his wings again". A poignant tale for all spiritual seekers, to rekindle their memories and inspire them to join their Brother and Sister Rays in the Sun.

LET me tell you what happened to me the last time I left the Sun — so begins the narrative of a Ray that went out from its home.

The Ray, i.e. a Wave of compassionate sentiments in the Heart of the Sun, has been given its essence and existence, has been created by the Great Ordainer, simply so that the universe will know that Love and Compassion exist. It is the ordained fate of this Wave to go out from the bosom of the Sun, along with all its myriad uncounted companions, the sisters and brothers born of the same parent, the one parent who is both their mother and father. These Waves of compassionate sentiments travel out through the whole universe, through all the open spaces. Wherever they touch becomes luminous. Whatever they touch, knows that it is. And before they touch, before these Waves, these Rays travelling out from the Sun touch an entity, the entity is but knows not that it is. So the first Grace that these Waves, these Rays travelling out from the Sun confer to entities is their own self-awareness, their own self-recognition. They travel out, touch and engulf, encapsule and surround, and bathe every object at a speed that cannot be gauged and measured by the slow motion of solid bodies. Planet after planet, stars after stars, every hidden cavity of space, and all things that dwell therein, are touched by their compassionate fingers, to become luminous, to become self-aware. The touch is so incredibly beautiful, from not knowing that one is, to know that one is; it is a leap that cannot be made without this touch of Grace. Only by their touch do we know that we are.

It is the nature of the impure, of the relatively impure, that it aspires to find a touch of the pure. Often in the process of that, we seduce the pure to become as impure as us. This is the incredible paradox of the interplay of spiritual and the material. The spiritual gives life to the material; the material deadens the spiritual, for, that is all that it has to give. We give only what we have. The material has nothing to offer but entropy, decay, death. So it rubs its dust on the luminous face of the Sun, wanting to turn the Sun to ashes so that it would be a companion to our ashes. Rare is the elevated soul who, upon touching the pure, wants to purify itself. Rare is the soul that upon encountering the serene, becomes serene, without seeking to impart its disturbance to that which is eternally quiet.

Long before you can experience serenity, long before you can quieten the mind, aspire that whenever you have been conferred the grace of the touch of the pure, you do not measure their speed with yours. That, you do not evaluate their eternity on the grounds of your entropy. Then gradually the fleeting touch will become a longer-lasting touch, and a deeper-infiltrating touch. The touch will then dwell within you. And that love will become a marriage.

There is this strange paradoxical love between the spiritual and the material. The spiritual wanting to make the material come alive; the material using the spiritual for its own purposes. Sometimes the pure seems to be temporarily seduced. "Oh hail!" It plays the game of being in love with that which it touches, for without that love, it cannot confer grace. Sometimes an identification is established between the two. With this background to my story, let me tell you what happened to me last time I left the Sun.

As I was encircling a solid body of matter, such gratitude arose from within that, which had now come alive,

> Tarry! Stay! Do not go further into the spaces beyond. For, without you I would go back to the oblivion of existence, simply being and not knowing of my own being, the darkness from which you have just elevated me, the deep well of oblivion from which you have just rescued me, pulled me up. Are you going to leave me and drop me back into that very well and make me mere matter again?

Such cry arose from that being to whom I had lovingly conferred awareness.

I cannot be bound to limitations. Brother Suns, Brother Rays, born of the same Parent; it is our fate to always wander, to always touch distant spaces that have not been touched before, to make things come alive, to dwell within them and yet not become them. But as all of us know at times, a certain identification is often established with those forms to which we have given life.

So it was that this time some force pulled me down. I gathered my vast unbound spaces, sought the centre of my expansiveness, withdrew my expansiveness into that point. And now I was no longer expansive as all the spaces of the universe; I was a mere point. And I entered this form, taking it as my dwelling place. I entered this form as a dwelling place, as an act of that natural love and compassion which has been ordained for us and we are fated to give, without counting how many times we have given awareness to how many forms; but, to actually make ourselves a pinpoint of light, no more expansive as the vast open spaces? What worse fate can befall any of us Rays than that we create thereby a world in which the darkness and Light have mingled, and so mingled that the darkness does not know where it ends and Light begins, and Light forgets where it ends and darkness begins?

How would I have known, never having been in darkness before, that when I have merged my being with this dark solid form, how diluted, how weakened I would feel? But let me warn you, my fellow Rays of Light, those of you who have never been sucked into the mire of darkness, when you confer your Love, your Light, your Grace, your Awareness, just confer it but never dwell. Never enter, never make that form your home, or else *immediately* your light will be diluted, you will be weakened. And if you still continue to dwell therein and do not immediately pull out, you will begin to identify yourself with that form. Then the darkness says, "I am Light", but the Light begins to say, "I am darkened". This is precisely what happened to me last time I left the Sun.

The Light that I am, began to cry out to the fellow Waves of Light passing by, "Pull me! Save me! Send a strand of your Grace and a streak of kindness to me who have become a solid form. Lift me just as I myself have done innumerable times through aeons upon aeons." They wrapped the solid form with Light and unwrapped, and then went on in their expansiveness, illuminating the vast spaces. Not pulling me out. For, have we not this awareness within our own nature, to know that it is only by our Self-will and Freedom of Will that we enter the solid darkened forms? And only by that Will can we again gather our strength and end this horror of dilution, and pull ourselves out again, and let darkness explode, and the journey continue, and the expansiveness be rediscovered?

Knowing this nature of myself — yet, I loved and I identified with this darkening solid, solid form — the Will to be free, the Will to recognize my freedom too was diluted, and the symptom of the dilution was that I sought the help of some other Grace — I who have always conferred Grace upon others. Ah, can You, who have never been touched by darkness even form an image of what it is to be so diluted, to be so darkened, to be so bound? To be a rock? To be a flesh? To be a bone, and not be a Wave of Light?

Within this solid form there were, oh, layers upon layers, just as here in our home there are layers upon layers of luminosities, the radiance of each layer unmatched and unique. Here were layers upon layers of ugly din, each slower moving than the other, in that temporary abode that I had chosen. The sense of heaviness there is incomparable. They call it gravity. These forms — they move, they move with a motion that here in the Sun would be considered as lying dead. These forms of darkness — they think that they think, but that thought to us is a worse fate than oblivion. Among them they speak of a hell full of fires, not knowing that fires are our heaven, and absence of fire is that hell where I have dwelt recently, I cannot say how long, for in that world there is no comprehension of our eternity.

Boundlessness is a mere word there. Oh, how I have suffered, for here among us, all are one and none alone. Here among us all being one, none is alone. But there was such total aloneness, because the Waves of Light passing by only touched the form, the dark solid, and something from within me would rise and aspire to go along, and yet by my imagination I had made a mere shadow my new identity.

Here in our Solar Realm when we Waves divide, each part is equally infinite, but in the finiteness of that darkness a division becomes smallness, yet smaller, yet smaller, more diluted, yet more diluted. The strength of Light wanes, and further wanes.

At times I was so weakened by this unnameable illness that I thought I too, like this material form, had actually died. That I, an Eternal Flame, confined to a frame had become extinguished, so little was my awareness. Yet a certain vague memory would linger of how I have given awareness of being to myriad forms. Yes, a certain vague memory would linger. Even in those moments of extinction, some particle of mine must have known that awareness is my nature and that extinction is totally alien to me.

Sometimes the remaining Will would impart an inspiration, and I would strengthen my self-awareness, and I would for brief moments come out of that seeming extinction. I had this weak hold on my consciousness, as I said. At times it was so weakened that, with regard to that flesh to which I had given sensation, I thought I was the sensation, and I was also the flesh. At times, in that cerebrum to which I had given vibration, I thought that I was its thought. I repeat, I had so identified myself with this form that dwelling in that cerebrum to which I had imparted my vibration, I thought that I was its thought.

But the Ordainer, the Great Source, the Sun who sends us forth, the Sun who shelters our solitude, the Sun from Whom we derive our serenity, does that Sun not know what fate had befallen its own creation, one of its own children? At times, ah, a vague memory would arise of my far away homeland and I would know that I am in exile. They would place before me all their golden feasts and tell me to feast on these for a lifetime, but they did not know that these feasts were not sufficient for me even to sup for an evening.

Knowing my deep unhappiness, a sense of loneliness that overpowered me, they would bring to me what they call dazzling lights, some forms that they would name diamonds, rubies. They would say, "Look at our sun, the moons, the stars!" But are these not lit by my Sister Rays? The sight of them would excite me, or something deep inside would stir that thought to which I had been reduced, with which I had been identified. That thought would say, "Yes, there is a vague memory of the emeralds that deck the staircase of my Imperial Palace". How could they even imagine that all of their stars and suns, all of their dazzling lights, rubies and diamonds gathered together from all of their universes cannot match a single strand of light from a single emerald that is bedecking the staircase to my Imperial Palace? The memory would pass like the flash of a long-gone love. Only a sigh remained, and other forms, whom you my Brothers and Sisters have graced, would say "Why, what is it you seek? Why are you not like us?"

They have a strange sense of normalcy down there. They would ask why it is that I did not conform to whatever it is that they consider to be their norm.

But it so happened — and here the upturn begins — one of you fellow Waves of Light passing by lingered a little longer.

Perhaps that is all I had needed. Suddenly it was as though my whole being went out, as though I had been touched again with pure unalloyed Luminosity that is our nature. It was as though I extended a hand to be lifted out of this dark well. But no I was not to be lifted, I was not to be saved by another. I must find my own recognition. But the touch of pure Light to the darkness-alloyed light that I had become was the initiation I had needed.

I know now that that touch lasted only a flash of a moment, but because it was a touch of Eternity I seemed to glimpse the whole of Eternity in that moment, and suddenly knew who I had been, who I truly was. My Will was recovered. I was not to dwell there long. The forms of solid matter would grab onto me, for they had claims on me. They said that I was indebted to them for all the blazing lights they had shown me — that I must repay my debt, that I must learn the norms of existence. As they said this to me, it meant that I must remain only a thought in the very cerebrum to which I had given all its vibration.

"Now, that is not to remain so!" I declared. "The walls of this prison must now be broken." I learned that if I simply remembered who I am, there was no more prison. That I must dwell on my Self-awareness, the Awareness of being the Wave of Light.

Longer and longer I would spend in the Awareness, and in that time the restless body would become still. And other bodies would look askance, and offer me medicines for my strange illness. They would kindly offer to analyse these "escapist" thoughts that were developing within me.

But even dwelling in that dark form, simply cultivating, letting flourish, letting nourish, the memory of my true being was ecstatic. Here you all and I, fellow Waves of Light, have the ecstasy as our norm. One does not go into It and come out. Perhaps that is why we are sometimes sent to those unecstatic worlds, so that by contrast, by contradistinction we would know how blessed we are.

It was in those short-lived moments of somewhat darkened and diluted ecstasy that I understood the distinction between Light and darkness, between the spiritual and the material. I understood why it is that every time we pass a material form and give it, not too long, a lingering touch, it seeks us out, reaches out, wishes to imprison us. Not out of malice to darken us too, but to make itself luminous. But my longings for my Original Nature wailed:

God, I lost what you gave me.
I lost my innocence.
Would you grant it to me again?
That when they curse me: "Idiot!"
I panic, wonder how they found out,
and renew diligent effort
to conceal that I am indeed a fool of God,
Oh God, make me your fool again.

That when they expel me: "Unclean!"
I am grateful they remind me in
what foul flesh-house I dwell
whose every opening oozes;
and renew effort to walk out free.
God, make me so pure again.

That when they reveal impassioned breast to
me I remember my own mother.
An infant to all women,
call out "Ma!" and cling to suckle. Mother, make
me your infant again.

God, I lost what you gave me.
Guide me to where I might find it again.

So at times I cried out and they said, "What beautiful poetry!" For they knew not the reality of that of what I spoke. Sometimes it would seem that fragrant breezes from my faraway Empire brought me the message of the Perfumes that the Flowers of my Land exude. If I suppressed the memory, then they among whom I had become a fellow form of stone, a heap of ashes, would rejoice. For they enjoyed, and they rejoiced each time I learned one of their ways. When the faraway breezes brought me the messages of the Perfumes that the Flowers of our Land exude they, the fellow citizens of the land of darkness, would present to me their own flowers. Bless our Maker, if you have never been subjected to such an imprisoned impassioned condition, for you cannot imagine what weak perfume they name as a flower. Who can know there that these mementos and souvenirs of our Land of Light have been strewn into their kingdom so that those of us who have the misfortune of ever being imprisoned there may again be reminded of their Home Kingdom.

Thus, for long I struggled. Whenever I recalled my true Being, darkness succumbed. The oblivion became oblivious of its oblivion and became a memory. The oblivion became oblivious of its oblivion and became an Awareness. The darkness was diluted and became Light. The stone-like form began to develop a certain vibrancy. Each time I would begin to succumb to darkness, I would remember those ecstatic moments, till one day, one of their days, Hmmmmm . . . .

Do you want to know how long one of their days is? It is as if you were to divide one of our days into a . . . . No, I cannot find a subdivision small enough to give you even a simile of how short their days, nay, their life-spans are, the life-spans to which they dearly cling, afraid of extinction. Let it pass. I do not wish to remember that suffering in smallness. Yet one day, one of their days, the memory became strong. Darkness crumpled upon itself, and I said to the solid stone clothing I wore:

> *Naked, I will dance in the Flames of the Sun, and with my arms open to hug the whole universe I will soar high in the skies.*
>
> *The blue ocean of sorrows is no more for me. The orange of the Light of Dawn will now welcome me to my own Land.*
> *I will deck my hair with all the stars,*

and the planets will be my stepping stones across the narrow stream of space.
My bridal night has come,
and there are no more veils for me.

I will lie in the arms of my Lover when I am weary of my cosmic dance,
and the twilight of the boundaries of this universe softly whispers in my ears with a smile that He awaits and the hour of union is nigh!

I am a maid of heavens, mortals.
Farewell. I have grown my wings again!

It was a stroke of fortune that you did not recognize me when I fell amongst you and clothed my limbs in shame,
embodied myself in shame,
with a body hid myself in shame
lest you tied me with the golden chains of your desires.

Farewell, my hosts on earth;
freed, I have laid myself bare again.
Farewell, mortals. I have grown my wings again!

Thus I left the world of darkness, but how can I not return there? For, knowing the sorrow of being a solid, the chief constituent of whose being is darkness, my compassion is even more heightened, now. Before this imprisonment I knew not what sorrows were veiled, hidden in these forms we barely touch and flit by. Now I have learned I must confer my Grace, even in greater intensity, and yet, at the same moment maintain yet greater centring of my Self-recognition, lest I be sucked again into the whirlpool, in the deep well of the darkness of the material world.

Fellow Waves of Light, we are all one, therefore none alone. What they call momentary ecstasies in the world of darkness is our perennial nature. Till you have lived in one of those stone prisons, you do not know how blessed we are as Eternal Souls.

Come, I hear a cry rising from distant worlds. Existences seeking Awareness. Come, I hear a cry from distant worlds, existences seeking Awareness. Come, let us proceed and compassionately confer to them the Awareness of their Being.

God, Sun, bless us on the journey.

11

Spheres of Light

> WE are beings of Light, bright beings, *deva*s, whose consciousness-energies have congealed into material forms. Beings of energy, of different vibrations, who have shaped themselves into natural forms in the Cosmic Dance, Cosmic Play, *līlā*. There are spheres within spheres, each layer vibrating at a different rate, with different time-senses, universal, planetary and variations of time clocks within the human personality like time zones of a planet. Often, beings continually look outward for the gold and jewels which are within, but in truth, some spheres of light, the Beings of Light, the great *siddha*s on this very planet have charged certain areas. You can go there (such as with the Kumbha Melās at the confluence of rivers), and you can feel the charge. So people call them Holy Places. There is also something in us, whom we playfully call human beings, that follows the gold rush, our own silver mines or collects diamonds or goes to the celebrations of sacred Light — because something in us draws, pulls and says: We absolutely must go there, herein!

THINK of a very, very thin silver foil and pass a little light through it. As it passes to the other side, look, not at the streak of silver, but at the light.

Or take a gold foil, very slim, and pass the light through that gold foil. Forget about the strip of gold; only remember the light.

Take a scoop shaped from crystal lightning, if you can, throw some diamonds in a luminous space. With the scoop, pick up their light.

Take all these lights and put them in a crystal container — only the lights, not the strips, not the foils, not the diamonds. Pick some rubies, amethysts and emeralds the same way and take *their* lights and pour into that crystal container — and mix this well.

Stand at the bank of a lake at sunrise, then look at the surface of the water and the way the sunlight red reflects. Stand at the ocean at sunset and skim from the surface of the sea the light of the sunset and from the surface of a lake the light of sunrise. Pour these lights also into the same crystal container. Stand at the same lake and the same ocean in the light of the full moon — forget the moon, forget the lake, forget the ocean, forget the water — only *skim* the light that reflects. Pour that also into that very crystal container. Mix it *well*. You are a Master Alchemist.

Out of that light, *only* the light, make a shape if you can. Only Beings of Light can. How that shape will shimmer and glimmer and how each non-particle wave of that light will contain itself — how many subtleties of colours which cannot be grasped, which cannot be held in hand are there! Do you know that you are that kind of a form? Somewhere along the line, these forms of such beautiful living light have caught particles of dust in their magnetic spheres. These particles of dust are your physical bodies, but these lights remain and make those dust particles shine.

You see someone walking on the street and you're struck dumb saying: Oh, how beautiful that person is. You say so only looking at the dust particles that are caught in the shape of these lights that you have imagined yourself gathering together and forming from them an Adam and an Eve, a Manu and Śatarūpā.[1]

The particles of dust cannot stay caught in those lights because the lights are living lights and these particles that are from dust can hardly be called living even though they glimmer, though they shimmer, though they play-act as though they were alive. But sooner or later, being alien to that frame of light — and don't you forget how beautiful those shapes are without the dust particles — sooner or later these dust particles drop off, and people around gather these dust particles, and bury them or cremate them, the funeral parlours making big business out of them. They are so valuable because they were once caught in a sphere of light. You are as those spheres of light, even though your bathroom mirrors only show the dust particles.

These living spheres of light are so vibrant that the slow, dull vibrations of our dust-particle eyes cannot see them. Even though the crystalline, silver, emeraldine, golden lights have converted these dust particles into the little crystals of our light and entered the little crystals of our eyes, our eyes simply cannot, never will be sharp enough, sensitive enough to see these shimmering, glimmering ever-vibrant dynamic Spheres of Light that, my reading friend, you are — and

---

[1] In the Indian tradition, Manu, the Mind-being of all *mantras* is the first Man. His wife is Śatarūpā, she of hundred beautiful forms. These together create all progeny, not in sin but as part of the Divine Being's creative play.

you, and also you — and the "you" sees a "you" and says, "You are as me". That we call love, because the lights recognize lights. However, when you are attracted only to the dust particles, there is no life in that love.

The ever-vibrant Spheres have *Will*. They can go faster or they can go slower. They can make themselves into many layers of lights. The central core-life of these spheres of light has the freedom of *Will* to shape itself, to become a dinosaur, to become an ant, to become a Cro-Magnon or the Homo-idiotic — busy uprooting trees, busy denuding the planet, busy plundering the gold mines because it is looking for its own nature. Busy plundering the gold mines because it is looking for its own nature in the wrong place, in the wrong acts. Busy becoming a billionaire to own all the diamonds, because it has forgotten: Greater than the light of all the diamonds of this earth, so far discovered and not discovered, is the light in the crystal container of their *Will*. The *Will* shapes the being, the diversity of life forms.

I know that the branch of zoology that is now very popular, called psychology, dealing with our animal nature — should I not call it a branch of zoology? — yes, dealing only with our animal nature, does not recognize these sphere of light, for, which dust-particle eyes have seen these lights? But I assure you, these spheres of light have a *Will* whereby they may shape themselves. They may change themselves into layers upon layers of light and at each layer that thus emanates from them may vibrate at a different level, different frequency. Do understand this part. They may shape themselves as they like, and they may divide themselves into many layers within the spheres, spheres within spheres.

In those spheres they may let a silver light predominate at one level, golden light scintillate at another level, the ruby-like light radiate at another level, an adamantine, diamond-like light play its luminous music at another level within the same sphere and all the different layers of light within the sphere, as we have said, may vibrate at different frequencies. Thereby they become *prāṇa* or individual unconscious or individual faculty of intelligence and wisdom (*buddhi*) or active operative mind. They become the channels incorporating the senses, the perceptive spheres and all of them, magnetized, remain together, remain as one sphere.

It is here that the masks made of dust particles say, "I am human!" "I am human!" "I am male!" "I am female!" "I am tall!" "I am large!" "I am small!" "I am tiny and puny!"

They may play-act as they like, for their self-will has made whatever shape they have chosen how to play, perform this joyous *līlā* (play); they learn how to play. One child says to the other child in its child *līlā*, "Look what I can do! Look how I can somersault so fast!" Just *līlā* — what's the purpose of that somersault? They enjoy their being. Being joyful, they play. When they play, they take these shapes and forms.

They have games they want to play — so they play! One acts a thief; the other acts a blind man. Whatever games they want to play, they play. The dust particle called the ant bites, the dust particle called the human. They play. Why do they play? Because they are playful. Why are they playful? Because they are joyful. Why are they joyful? Because they are beings of light — nothing wanting, nothing missing, nothing to be unhappy about. One plays a teacher, the other plays a student. It's a game you and I are playing. When they let the different layers of the spheres of light vibrate at different levels and frequencies with different types of light predominating, then those become the various faculties: senses, *prāṇa*, mind, the five *kośa*s, and three bodies and so on and so forth. The *suṣumṇā*, and the *iḍā*, and a *piṅgalā* and 72,000 energy-currents — "only 72,000?! No, I'll make it 125,000. Okay! 125,000! Fine!" Do you follow? That is how this universe has come into being.

Each of these levels within the spheres of light have a different time-sense. The body works at one kind of time and the breath works at another; the *prāṇa* works at a different kind of time. The different levels of mind work at different types of time. That's why you can dream as though 24 hours or 24 years have elapsed. When you open your eyes, it was less than five minutes because different levels, the planes within the individual spheres of light, vibrate at different frequencies, and therefore they have different "stretch", as it were, different measures, varying measures, of time. The same applies to the vast mega-sphere called the Universe. So that when I want something done — today's what, Thursday? — when I'm sitting in a town called Rishikesh and it is Thursday evening and I want something done in Minneapolis on Thursday morning, I send my messages from Rishikesh on Thursday evening, and it arrives yet on that Thursday's morning and the work gets done during that day. Yeah! While I'm sleeping Thursday night, they are working in USA on Thursday daytime. To one who has not travelled, this is just a fascinating statement.

Imagine now the time zones of the gigantic moons of mega-planets around uncountable trillion stars in another uncountable trillion galaxies, and those innumerable ones in countless universes after universes. How many time zones are there in God? God is aware of all of those times all at once, and a liberated soul learns to play across those enormous networks of time zones; s/he talks today of six Manu-intervals hence as though that supposed "future" were here today. At times I have been scolded by the Master for mistakes I have not yet committed and find myself committing the same many years later. Then I remember the scolding and restrain myself from making the mistake.

Some who have gathered the dust particles in their play have begun to take these dust particles a little too seriously. I'm sure you recognize those few around some place. Some wear the dust particles playfully, and some wear them so that they can, every now and then, remind the others:

"Come on, come on, come on! Don't take these dust particles too seriously, okay? That's not what you really are, huh?"

"Really? Oh! I should talk in wonderful poems!"

"No, I'm not talking in poems."

"Oh, this is very profound philosophy." Many write the history of philosophy and praise Pythagoras here and Socrates there and Emmanuel Kant somewhere else, and start memorizing and writing examinations on philosophy, writing doctoral theses, filling tomes and occupying libraries' shelves. After a couple of hundred, couple of thousand years, an ignorant tyrant comes along and burns those libraries; the history of philosophy starts all over again. Then what was Pythagoras doing, and what was Socrates saying, and what was Emmanuel Kant stating? What purpose could they have to give work to us poor, twenty-first-century students to go through all of that analysis. Now you can have an analysis through a computer of the language of Emmanuel Kant. And, what did he say? All these philosophers seem to say, "Hey, you are not a dust particle; you are a sphere of light!" Today someone does a computer analysis of the sentence and becomes a great professor of philosophy, yet not suspecting that his real name is Prof. Sphere of Light PhD!

Here and there, these spheres of light, the beings of light, the great *siddha*s have charged certain areas on this very planet. You can go there and feel the charge. So people call them "holy places". There is something in us, whom we playfully call human beings, that follow the gold rush, our own silver mines or collects diamonds or goes to the celebrations of sacred light — because something in us draws, pulls, and says "Let's go there, herein!"

Hence the ancient *ṛṣi* prayed:

asato mā sad gamaya
tamaso mā jyotir gamaya
mṛtyor mā amṛtam gamaya

Lead me from the non-existent unreal to the truly eternally existent Real;

Lead me from darkness of the ignorance of self-nature to the light of self-knowing;

Lead me [thus] from my [illusion of] death to realization of [my] non-mortality.

— *Bṛhadāraṇyaka Upaniṣad* 1.3.28

When they opened their eyes from *samādhi*, they could not but proclaim:

jyotiḥ! jyotiḥ! jyotiḥ!

Light! Light! Light!

The word *jyotiḥ* is repeated in the *Ṛgveda* 307 times.

idam vai tan madhu

This is indeed that honey;
This is indeed that mead! (Repeated four times)
— *Bṛhadāraṇyaka Upaniṣad* 2.5.16-19

In the *saṁnyāsa* (renunciation ceremony[2] of Swami vows) one prays nine times:

May I become [a being of] light.
— *Mahā-Nārāyaṇa Upaniṣad* 20.15-21, 24, 25

So brilliant a light; so sweet a mead.

Such beings of light whose very being is a sweetest mead, when they have to roam around among the light-infused statuettes shaped of dust particles, us humans, just to remind us of our nature, their exile carries a cosmic compassion as well as a cosmic sadness.

After my Master had shown me the light, once I asked him: *Gurudeva*, how do you manage to stay away from your world of Light and roam in this world? His voice carried a profound cosmic sadness and he said, "Do not remind". That sigh, I am sure was heard by those of the *siddha* hierarchy whose emissary he was. Finally they called him back, leaving us sighing.

Here I share a composition from nearly forty years ago:

The earth is a light, the sky is a light, the beauty of your skin, the softness of your child's cheek, the love in your eyes is a light. The light has become a leaf, a twig, a tree. Light flows as a river from a mountain of

---

[2] For complete (somewhat summarized) translation of this ceremony, ask ahymsinpublishers@gmail.com

light. Whatever you do not experience is not light. All the rest is waves in a sea of light, the light that is the Infinite delight, the bliss of God.

The lake of Truth and the mirage of falsehood is all light. The song you hear is a light to your ears; the sweet taste is a light to your palate; love is the light of heart; as meditation is the light of your soul.

Light wears many garments and of these your prayer and your *mantra* is the brightest.

The sound that is the wave of the universe, the word that is the soul of God is your inner light, wearing the body which is an outer layer of light.

Why would you worship darkness when your eyes are made to see only light?

Set aside your dark angers, and your deep depressions. Hold still for a moment, fellow wave of light. Be still. Do you see how the winds of your agitations calm down and the resolute light illumines your mind again.

On the altar of the light of true knowledge burn the light of love.

On this day may you walk as a being of light. Wherever you tread leave your footprints of light. Let light alone be your delight. Light![3]

May you taste the sweetness of this honey-thick light. Wherever you walk, walk as a luminous being with no darkness left, no doubts remaining, nothing yet to desire or conquer.

May your meditations prosper.

---

[3] First published in *Light of Ten Thousand Suns*, YES Publishers, St. Paul, MN.1999; Full Circle, New Delhi, 2001. Available from ahymsinpublishers@gmail.com

12

Ladder of the Thunderbolt

Christ said, "Enter through the narrow gate. For wide is the gate and broad is the road that leads to destruction, and many enter through it. But small is the gate and narrow the road that leads to life, and only a few find it" (*Matthew* 7:13-14). Such is the "razor's edge" of the Path of the Thunderbolt, the Dorje Path of the Tibetan Buddhists, Jacob's Ladder for the Christians, also the ladder of St. John Climacus (He of the Ladder). So also St. John of the Cross sings of the *Ascent of Mount Carmel*. To do it you need two things, a "push" and a "pull". "Pushing" yourself by aspirations, love and service and receiving the *guru*'s "pull". The Path of the Thunderbolt is also seen in Tibetan pilgrims ascending the steps of the Potala on their knees, and in verses from *The Divine Comedy* where Dante speaks of his love for the Divine Beauty, Beatrice.

Below is edited transcript of a lecture following a guided meditation.

As we were meditating, where we were a few moments ago and as we often do, we go through the exercise of ascent and descent along the path of the breath. This path, in the traditions of Tibet, is called the *vajra* path, *vajra* being a Sanskrit word. The Tibetan expression is *dorje* path, the Path of the Thunderbolt, path of *upāya*, that is, the method for ascent. One who has mastered this path is called a Vajra Master, the

Thunderbolt Master, the Master of the Thunderbolt.

Now, we know the place that the thunderbolt has occupied in many cultures of the world, from the Nordic mythology to Tibetan mysticism. The thunderbolt is always said to be a weapon of some god of light. The Sanskrit word for a god of light is "shining one", *deva,* a word closely related to *dieu*, as in *adieu*, or *dios* or *theos*, and many such words in Indo-European languages. It is a God-given gift that we too can become holders and wielders of the thunderbolt, become *deva*s, shining ones. The weapon, *par excellence,* of Indra, the king of gods as the masterful soul, is *vajra* in the Vedic traditions. It is with this *vajra* that Indra vanquishes the demon of cosmic darkness.

The purpose of all spiritual aspiration is to become as a god. The Christian mystics have said, "God became man so that man, in him, may become God" in what Greek mystics called "*opotheosis*".[1] One who is a Vajra Master walks on what is known as Vajradhara, the Stream of the Thunderbolt, the sharp sword-like edge of the Thunderbolt. He has to walk, as Jesus said, on "the straight and the narrow". The Upaniṣads exhort us:

uttiṣṭhata jāgrata prāpya varān ni-bodhata kṣurasya dhārā |
ni-śitā dur-atyayā durgam pathas that kavayo vadanti | |

Arise! Awake! Finding the boon-granting preceptors, become aware!

---

[1] Jesus answered them, "Is it not written in your Law, 'I have said you are gods'" (John 10:34-35). Cf. "I have said, ye are gods; and all of you are children of the most High" (Psalms 82:6).

> Sharp is the razor's edge, difficult to get across. The poets of wisdom call it a path difficult to traverse.
>
> — *Kaṭha Upaniṣad* 1.3.14

On this, Śaṅkarācārya says (paraphrased here):

> You have been sleeping the sleep of ignorance of self-nature. Arise from it. Wake up and turn to self-knowledge. Attain the awareness of *ātman* the spiritual self.
>
> For this you are required to traverse the path of an extremely subtle faculty of wisdom (*buddhi*), a path that is not easy to cross because of its subtlety.

Razor's edge is *prajñā*, the realization of wisdom and is coupled with *vajra*, the method through which the preceptors guide us. A prime step in this method is the mastery of *prāṇa*. The Upaniṣad says:

> All this moving universe emanates [from and] trembles, vibrates, moves in *prāṇa*;
>
> This [*prāṇa*] is the great awesome raised [weapon that is] *vajra* the thunderbolt.
>
> Those who know it become immortals.
>
> This is the way to becoming shining ones, immortal *devas*.

Because on this earth we walk on a horizontal path, the images presented to us by these terms suggest to our thus-habituated minds that the spiritual walk is also a horizontal walk from here to there. We have subjected ourselves to the binding chains and shackles of the finitude of the time–space co-ordinate called the physical body, we think that because our physical body walks horizontally on the firm ground, all walks are horizontal. But ask a gecko that walks up the wall. Ask a bird that sometimes soars straight up. Its path is not bound to a horizontal conception of space and time. Those who walk on the eternity of that lightning, whose horizons are infinite, that lightning which is a thunderbolt wielded by the shining ones, learn to walk like the shining ones without the limitations of horizons, therefore they do not walk horizontal. Their walk is the walk of an internal, inward ascent and descent, not walking to and fro, but ascending and descending. Whenever you read of a walk in the spiritual realm, therefore, do not think horizontal, think of the ascent and descent, or better still, inward and outward, and yet better, a walk that is stillness.

On such a path, one covers all the possible realms that a mystic can explore. Since our consciousness has become bound to limitations, quite often we cannot climb straight up along the edge of this sword, this sharp sword, this razor's edge. Somerset Maugham, in writing the novel based on the Upaniṣadic passage on the razor's edge, may not have realized that the razor's edge is not horizontal, that it is the path of spiritual ascent and descent. But we have not learned to climb straight along the edge of this sharp *vajradhara*, the sword and the thunderbolt wielded by gods, who also dwell within us. Every now and then they reveal their presence. Every now and then they reveal their shining, brilliant presence, in strange places, in crowded places and in wilderness equally, so long as one remains in solitude even in a crowd, in what the *sūfīs* of the Naqshbandi Order call *khalwat dar anjuman*, solitude in crowd.

People complain: Sometimes we don't want to go to meditate at a meditation centre because we are used to solitude and it's so crowded at the centre. Have you ever been lonely in a crowd? If you have been lonely in a crowd, why can you not experience solitude in a crowd? In this space where you are sitting, nobody else is sitting. How big a space do you want for your solitude? So, whether in a crowd or in a wilderness, wherever you have solitude the shining ones reveal themselves. St. John Climacus says:

> The cell of a hesychast[2] is the body that surrounds him and within him is the dwelling place of knowledge.
> — *The Ladder of the Divine Ascent,* Step 27

Jacob on his way to find his bride, lay down, put a stone under his head and slept as he was very tired — we read in the Book of Genesis, chapter 28. He dreamt of a ladder, of angels ascending and descending. The ladder of spiritual awakening has many steps, as many steps as you want to assign to it. Some say eight, some say seven, some say six. St. John Climacus (He of the Ladder) wrote his treatise[3] about the thirty steps of the spiritual ladder. It starts with the first step, renunciation, and ends with the thirtieth step of love. His twenty-seventh step being *hesychea*, stillness.

St. John of the Cross has given us *The Ascent of Mount Carmel* and has drawn an architectural map of the path to the highest peak. He proceeds, as in the Yoga tradition, abandoning all claims to earthly as well as heavenly pleasures, saying at each step "not this", "not this", till one reaches where "only the honour and glory of God dwells on this mount". But to reach that one has to start with a dark night of the soul which is stated:

> *One dark night,*
> *Fired with love's urgent longings*

---

[2] A meditative practitioner of stillness.

[3] *Ladder of the Divine Ascent* of John Climacus, Paulist Press, New York, 1982.

Ah, the sheer grace! —
I went out unseen,
My house being now all stilled.[4]

St. John explains this dark night of the soul as threefold. One, abandonment of involvements with the senses. Two, surrendering intellect to faith. Three, finally reaching God, the highest peak of the mountain.

Some can make the direct leap or can leap across one or two steps at one time — if you have the flight in you, if you have the lift!

For ascending, you need two things: you need a lift, and you need a pull. The lift comes from you, and the pull comes from the *gurus*, the guides, the angels, the prophets, the spiritual beings who are always calling and saying, "Come. Come here. Come here. It's beautiful up here. It's brilliant. It's a splendour. We cannot explain in words, even in inspirations, only in experience. Come here. Let us show you."

Every now and then the whisper is heard. As we see in Swami Rama's book, *Love Whispers*.[5]

He has dedicated this book to Her. He speaks of Her serenity, source of inspiration, that light — page after page. Some are short pieces, some are long pieces. He sings of "My Phantom Lady" and the "Love Offering", and "Golden Footprints", and his "Resolution", that quenching of thirst, and that "Separation is Brutal", and yet how the "Vessel of Life" may be filled in an "Eternal Communion". He speaks of

---

[4] *John of the Cross: Selected Writings*, ed. Kieran Kavanaugh, Paulist Press, New York, 1987.

[5] *Love Whispers* of Swami Rama, Himalayan Institute, Honesdale, Pa., 1986.

"Thou Art Inexplicable". He speaks of his "Exalted Love", his "Flow of Love", and "Blossoms Dropped by the Night".

Someone may have asked him, "what do you do?" so he replies:

What do you do?

I pick up the blossoms dropped by night,
I listen to the whispers of silence.
I contemplate on the vast void within.
I babble her name in each breath of my life.
I revere the beauty of her radiant face.

When sun comes out of bed, I retire
I enter the depths of void and bathe in the eternal fire.
Through clouds of joy,
The windless bird of my spirit soars higher and higher.
I am in love and fused beyond desire.

That is what I do.

Is She, the one of Whom Swami Rama sings, the same as Sophia of the *Books of Wisdom* in the Bible, Umā Haimavatī of *Kena Upaniṣad*, Dante's *Beatrice*?

So this "whispers from above and whispers from below": the lift and pull. Pulls in many different ways. Pulls on as many different heartstrings as you have. Some have only one and produce a monotone. Some have seven. Some have three. Some have twenty-seven. Some have 108. How many strands is the necklace you wear? By that many strands you are pulled. Some are pulled because they are mothers. Some are pulled because they are children. Some are pulled because they are infants. Some because they are adults. Some are pulled because they are very poor. Some are pulled because they are rich and must be taught to scatter their riches.

The great Ramaṇa Maharṣi pulled many people in many

different ways. Every night he would wake up at 2 a.m. and cut vegetables for the *āśrama*, because only he knew who might be visiting the *āśrama* next day. He would prepare just that much. He calls his cook one afternoon and says: Prepare food for two; two hungry people are coming. He pulled them by their hunger. There was a woman who saw him, a young sage not seeking anything, sitting hours in *samādhi*, worms crawling over him, body becoming emaciated daily. She started bringing him food. One day he's in one cave; another day he's in another valley. For fifty years of his life, this woman cooked daily and searched for him, and when she found him, fed him. In what valley he is today? In what cave he is? She would search, walk through all his haunts and places where he might be found. Sometimes she searched the whole day, but made sure that some food went into him. For fifty years this woman did that for a sage. And my! What stories she had to tell of him! He pulled her by her mother's maternal heartstrings. The sage's body was kept together.

So, some are pulled because they have service in them. Others are pulled because they have love in them. Others are pulled because they have words in them, and by the word-strings they are pulled. Find the place where you feel the pull, and right there also you will feel the lift. That, my friends, is really the true meaning of levitation. It is only from within you that you can feel both the lift and the pull. You will find your path; you will find your rung of the ladder.

So, many things happen on these ladders. Sometimes you would see pilgrims in India walking up a narrow mountain path to a temple, high up, on their knees, all the way up, climbing up on their knees. You can see that in Rome sometimes — all those steps. The great Sun Temple built by Marcus

Aurelius, the emperor, later converted to a cathedral. How many steps there are? And you see pilgrims in this day climbing up on their knees. You see that in old Tibet, pilgrims coming from all over Tibet and climbing up the steps of the Potala Palace in prostration. I have seen pilgrims in Korea do the same, and I hear, in Japan. In India it is a common sight.

The path up the spiritual ladder is a very pleasant one, but not always physically comfortable. It's a very pleasant path, because its pleasures are known only to those who walk on it. And then — the light! There is that light, the vision of which you have seen someplace, somewhere. A light that has been promised to you out of darkness. Like a traveller lost in the valley, not knowing where to go, who sees a flickering candle somewhere in the distance and starts walking in that direction. Like that. It has been promised; it has been shown. Once it has been shown, you have no alternative. You are drawn. You cannot go this way or that way, whether you have to go over a brook or a stone or a rock or over a mountain or over a valley or over thorns or over pebbles. You are drawn. Some magnet hides in that star-spark, and you just keep going, and you keep going, and you just keep going, whether your body remains or your body drops on the way. That Light! in the words of Walt Whitman in *Leaves of Grass*, in the prayer of Columbus:

> *That thou, oh God, my life has lighted with ray of light, steady, ineffable, vouchsafed of Thee,*
>
> *Light rare, untenable, lighting the very light, beyond all signs, descriptions and languages.*
>
> *For that, o God, be it my latest word here on my knees, old, poor and paralysed, I thank thee.*

Saint Gregory of Palamas, speaking of the transfiguration of Christ, extols the Taboric light, the light of the Mount

Tabor: the uncreated character of that Divine Light.

Dante in *Divine Comedy* seems to touch upon the glory of the light of *kuṇḍalinī* and its *suṣumṇā* stream. He sings in *El Paradis*:

> *E vidi lume in forma di rivera . . .*
>
> *I saw light in the form of a river*
> *Radiant light, reddish-gold*[6]
> *Between two banks*
>
> *Painted with wondrous spring [colours].*
>
> *From such a flooding stream there emerged live sparks that settled on the flowers all around like rubies circled by gold.*
>
> — *Canto* XXX.61-66

This is one of the most poetic depictions of *kuṇḍalinī* and of the flowers (*cakra* lotuses in full spring) found anywhere. The two banks between which *suṣumṇā* flows are indeed *iḍā* and *piṅgalā*, the left and the right streams of living energy.

Again, about the "vivo lume", the living light, he says:

> *Ne la profonda e chiara sussistenza . . .*
>
> *Out of that profound and bright sustenance*
> *of the light on high appeared to me three circles of light,*
> *of three different colours but of a single continency . . .*
>
> — XXXIII.114-16

---

[6] Tawny, is translated as reddish-gold by Allen Mandelbaum, 1984. In the context of a spiritual light, that indeed is a more appropriate translation. We have modified his translation for our own context (only here). Actually reddish gold (*aruṇā*) is the colour in which the universal Divine Mother is visualized in major Sanskrit hymns addressed to Her.

Further,

> *O luce eterna che sola te sidi . . .*
>
> *O eternal Light that dwell solely in yourself,*
> *Only you know you*
> *Self-knowing, self-known*
> *You love and smile upon yourself.* —XXXIII.124-26

There is white, red and blue of which you hear in the songs of Indian mystics, like the great lady mystic singer of Kashmir known as Lalla Dêd who sang of Three Circles of Light. The last lines we have quoted from Dante echo the Upaniṣadic *ātma-jyotiḥ, ātma-ratiḥ*: self-luminous and self-delighting *ātman*, the spiritual self.

This is the path of light, the path of the thunderbolt, the path in which descent is no descent at all. What descends is the energy that pulls and thereby becomes an ascent. What descends is the energy that reaches down and pulls. When the mother stoops to pick up the falling child, she is not going through the process of falling. Her descent is your ascent. This is how the lower *cakra*s push the energy upwards and the higher ones pull the same up,[7] like the sap rising in a tree. And here the up and the down then become one.

Dive. Climb. Be still.

I wish you a Thunderbolt and a climb up the Ladder.

---

[7] See this author's *Philosophy of Hatha Yoga* as well as audio-recordings on *kuṇḍalinī* and *cakra*s. ahymsinpublishers@gmail.con

13

Thousand Names of Kuṇḍalinī

A Blessing and a Grace: Two Conversations with Gurudeva

1. Gurudeva said: Son, let me grant you some *siddhi*s. The disciple replied: Gurudeva, I have no desire for *siddhi*s; grant me *samādhi* if it can be so granted to me. The *guru* looked pleased but said nothing.

2. Later, some years later:

Gurudeva (in Hindi): Son, at least ask me for something.
Disciple: *ṛṣitva*.

(I recall uttering only this one word, meaning "the *ṛṣi* status".)

Gurudeva: Granted.

(He uttered just this one word, in English). I joined my hands and bowed in gratitude.
Meditation grants one realization of an inner fullness. This fullness renders one helpless with grace received in the form of what others may call "creativity" but what is the full-time engagement of *ṛṣi*s, the "seeing", *darśana*, unravelling ever "new" depths of reality.

In such a state of being, thoughts that arise are not concepts nor fantasies but the insights helplessly granted. These insights don garments of words as they traverse the paths of mind starting from "vision" at the internal, transcendent end and concluding on the grosser and externalized end in speech.

These revelations become *mantra*s.

The words gathered in this composition are not mine. I am only the helpless transcriber of what was granted as grace. They appeared at all hours and in all different conditions, when the meditative background was the strongest in the mind. Then they were written down.

At the time of receiving there was no concept of metrical symmetries. They were *guru* corded as received and a number of verses "suffer" *chando-bhaṅga* (asymmetry of metres). I have not dared to "correct" and re-compose them.

Translating from Sanskrit is a challenge. The idiom of a business language does not match the idiom of the language created for transcendental philosophy. One needs to write so many footnotes to convey the semblance of a sense of so many words. That I have attempted to do.

Nearly 3,000 names were received in this gushing fountain. To conform to the textual traditions of other similar Sanskrit texts I have called the composition "Thousand Names". Of these only 109 are translated here.[1] Those who know the meaning of a *japa-mālā* (rosary used for *mantra* remembrance that has 108 beads plus one *meru* or *guru* bead) will understand why the number is 109.[2] The remaining ones could not be easily rendered into English.

---

[1] For original Sanskrit words, please see the author's Sanskrit composition, *Devo-duthi,* available at ahymsipublishers@gmail.com

[2] For further explanation see this author's *Mantra and Meditation,* available from ahymsinpublishers@gmail.com

Even those names that have been rendered into English here are approximations. Let us take the following rendering:

> Who is worshipped by a billion frolicking beautiful celestial nymphs who bear the bodies made of light of the pathways of energy-channels coursing through the great groves that flourish inside the jewel of the minutest point (*bindu*).

These thirty-seven words are approximate rendering of a thirteen-member compound word[3] in the original:

> *aniṣṭha-maṇi-bindv-antar-mahodyān-stha-mañjari-nadī-patha-pr-bhā-dehi-sundarī-koṭi-rādhitā* |

Its compact mental associations that go with each member word, nor the tonal rhythm, can be conveyed here. Similarly,

> Who nurses on her breast the infants that are the immeasurable universes

is a translation of six succinct words:

> *ananta-akhaṇḍa-viśva-aṇḍa-śiśu-dhātrī* |

Those, however, in whom the *kuṇḍalinī* has been awakened to whatever degree, in them She will inspire the meanings of Her names.

May it be so for you.

* * *

A boundary river flows between the regions of "Is" and "Is Not".

---

[3] For those not familiar with this concept in language, a compound word is a composition of many words which, only together, yield an intended meaning. For example, "father-in-law" is a compound word. German is rich in such compound words but in Sanskrit there may be a compound word with a thousand component members which together yield a meaning.

Among its waves perhaps there is, or is not, a tiny ray-endowed ripple.

The ripple's minutest centre point is the gateway to enter another world that is

- beyond spaces
- place of 'Solo' (*kaivalya*),
- dweller inside the *Brahman*-Void (transcendent Null, *śūnya*).

In its no-time time is neither aeoned[4] nor epoched by those who stay in the non-altering[5] consciousness, they

- who bear no names nor forms,
- who have reached the end of the pacification of space and time, that is, who have pacified space and time to their end.

There a sage named *a-nāmā*[6] entered the central point of the ripple, and reached trans-locale solitude of a world–non-world whose sky is a lightning.

There he projected his own lightning brilliance.

Of this, his own lightning brilliance, he shaped the ceiling, walls and floors, creating a cottage made of this light.

Therein he dwells in delight, self[7]-delighting (*ātma-rati*),

[4] Aeoned, epoched, neologisms, nominal verbs formed from nouns aeon and epoch. The two words translated here from Sanskrit mean that there are neither cycles of creations and dissolutions of the universes (*kalpa* = aeon) nor the sub-divisions (*yuga* = epoch) therein that normally last billions of years in the Hindu cosmology.

[5] Very rough translation of *nirvikalpa*, the highest *samādhi* in which no alternating mind-waves arise.

[6] Nameless.

[7] Not ego-self but *ātman*-self throughout this composition.

self-glorious, having renounced *buddhi*[8] and staying in *samādhi*.

There his Selfness-self frolics in the Consciousness-space, neither of pain nor of pleasure.

Now, his previous good disciples

- still living in some common world,
- still stuck in the ground of "Is" and "existent", bearing the ego-I awareness,
- not seeing their preceptor,
- became agitated of mind.

Then, some of them abandoned that Retreat (*āśrama*) that had been created from the *guru*'s power and wandered here and there, their minds caught in spaces and times for lack of intelligence.

Among them, however, was one disciple who had placed his intelligence into the Self, desiring to rise from names and forms but not succeeding in his climb on his own.

The *guru* had at one time laughingly given him the epithet *sa-nāmā*[9] before initiating him in the entry into Point.[10]

This disciple missing his *guru*, reminiscing and remembering of the *guru*'s mind unceasingly, tuned his mind-

---

[8] *Buddhi*, the first and the subtlest product of Ur Nature (*prakṛti*), the faculty of intelligence that is left behind in the highest *samādhi* for *ātman* to dwell in eternal self-knowing.

[9] One who still has a name, as contrasted with *guru*'s epithet of *a-nāmā*, nameless.

[10] A special *yoga* initiation whereby one may enter the central minute point of consciousness through which one will later burst into transcendent realm.

field into that of the *guru* and entered the cognitive *samādhi*.[11]

There,

- his awareness settled in *guru-cakra*,[12] remembering the *guru* therein,
- at the banks of the lake of the waters of silence,
- at the footsteps of the interior Kailāsa,[13] he meditates, and chants the *mantra* of which only the rare disciple is worthy:

śrīṁ gurave namaḥ |

As he thus unceasingly remembered the *guru* and meditated upon the *guru*'s force, the *guru* heard the pleas of this contemplative monk (*muni*) with consciousness-ear.

Knowing this senior disciple qualified and endowed with capacity, to cut asunder his binding nets of name, form, objects, space and time within a short moment, the *guru* drew the disciple to himself by the power of his brilliance and by the grace of *abhi-dhyāna*,[14] and set the disciple's mind-field into his own cottage made of lightning.

He said to him with a silent voice, whose form is a vibration of brilliance:

---

[11] *Samprajñāta*, the penultimate *samādhi* which still has one interior object to concentrate on whereas the a-cognitive, *a-samprajñāta*, has no more object.

[12] A particular centre of consciousness an entry into which confers connection with the universal *guru* and one's own *guru*.

[13] The holy mountain in Tibet, held most sacred by followers of four religions, the abode of Śiva. In this composition the sacred mountain is within oneself.

[14] Whereby God meditates upon the devotee and the *guru* meditates upon the disciple to confer grace.

As you have perfected the pleasantness of mind, maintained the practice of the presence of God, your momentum of progress is strong with your mind ever surrendered to the *guru*, and thus you have been calling me unceasingly, repeatedly prostrating to me with your mind.

I have therefore pulled you by my power of attraction here and brought you to this non-*āśrama* located in Void, brilliant with the stream of the energies of space consisting of consciousness.

Indeed, I will tell you all that you desire to know; I will remove your doubts.

Ask, ask, you clear-minded one.

That disciple named *sa-nāmā* then seeing himself transported thereto, with an amazed mind, replied:

Fathomless is your grace.

I prostrate again and again and inquire.

How may one enter from *samprajñāta*[15] into *dharma-megha*?[16]

How may I attain that "solo" state of *a-sam-pra-jñāta* which is attainable only by those like yourself?

Hearing this, that preceptor whose form was pure brilliance, entering *sa-nāmā*'s consciousness, inspired this wordless message into that disciple's *buddhi*:

---

[15] Cognitive *samādhi* in which only a single ideation remains as the object of concentration.

[16] A higher level of *samprajñāta, samādhi* of the Raincloud of Virtue and of the Knowledge of All Things. For further explanation see this author's commentary on the *Yoga Sūtras* of Patañjali, available from ahymsinpublishers@gmail.com

> This coiled energy, *kuṇḍalinī*, that is within you has as its nature the Vast (*virāṭ*).[17]
>
> Enter her, dwell in her, who is
>
> - subtle and slim like a lotus fibre, of the nature of lightning, and
> - streams of myriad brilliant colours, as if a line of rays drawn.

When you will ascend and descend within her on the paths of exhalation and inhalation, with intelligence one-pointed with the *mantra*,

> Then this thousand-named ladder of *yoga* will lead you with untrembling haste to the heaven that is in the cottage of Consciousness.

Sa-nāmā said:

> I will indeed embark on this path of *yoga* with reverence. But do tell me:
>
> This *kuṇḍalinī* of which you, revered preceptor, speak, what are its thousand names?

Thus asked by *sa-nāmā*, *a-nāmā* the preceptor who consists only of pure consciousness, replied:

> The meaning, reality and essence of these names can be obtained only through deep contemplation; thereafter by meditation, and then through *śakti-pāta*.[18]

---

[17] The Universe as the manifested body of God, explained in the *Bhagavad-Gītā*, chapters 9-11.

[18] A very high initiation wherein the *guru*'s consciousness-energy is transfused into that of the disciple, giving the latter a transcendental view of the reality of the universe, of his own personal self and of the Ultimate Reality. There are many degrees of *śakti-pāta*, depending on the disciple's capacity and power to absorb and assimilate the energy.

As the *yogin* progressively sees the highest of lightnings within his frame, so does he receive revelation of the secret of the *virāṭ*-self.[19]

Then all the sciences and arts come of their own accord to that *śakti-yogin.*[20]

One then conquers the three *śakti*s,[21] that is, all the *śakti*s concealed in the secret chamber. Then one comes to know the hidden meaning of the names.

I shall now recite to you thousand and more names of *kuṇḍalinī* in a billionth part of a micro-moment as I cast a ray of light into you.

Within that fraction of a moment this knowledge will enter your meditative *buddhi.*

Then stabilized in that *ātma-śakti,* the celestial *kuṇḍalinī,* by *a-sam-pra-jñāta samādhi*[22] you will be the self of your self and dweller of the self. Know that to be *kaivalya* — absolute solitude, *nirvāṇa* — a blowing out, *mokṣa,* the supreme liberation.

Then this *kuṇḍalinī* will become your very self and you the lightning-self of consciousness.

You will see that secret in the *virāṭ*-egg[23] as well as in yourself.

---

[19] *Virāṭ* is explained in a note above. Here, that very Vast being of the universe is seen as one's own self.

[20] One who practices *śakti-yoga* whereby all the *śakti*s, network of energy patterns, become real to one.

[21] All *śakti*s, potentials of the Omnipotent, are categorized into three: *icchā-śakti* (the power of volition), *jñāna-śakti* (power of knowledge) and *kriyā-śakti* (power of creation and creativity and action).

[22] A-cognitive *samādhi* in which all ideation is transcended.

[23] One of the words for the universe, *brahmāṇḍa, Brahman-*

→

> Having reached this pedestal you will then dissolve into *Brahman*.

Then did the *guru* radiate a pure bright ray of consciousness-*śakti* into the consciousness of the disciple within a billionth of a micro-moment.

There arose intuitions in the disciple's consciousness, with ease and naturally, effortlessly, together with all the concealed secrets.

He saw the fullness of all from the root of the *cakra*s all the way to *Brahman*-egg of the whole universe.

Later, descending from *paśyantī* to *madhyamā*[24] speech, he taught the same to his mind-born[25] disciples.

They in turn passed this knowledge to their own disciples.

That knowledge thus passed on in the lineage, we received as a flash in a moment in our consciousness and, filled with compassion we transfer it on to those desirous of liberation.

→ egg, because of the imagery of the universe being like an enclosed egg. The same is referred to here as *virāṭ*-egg.

[24] In the Indian philosophy of language there are four levels of language. The highest is the transcendental, *parā*, a pure spiritual experience beyond thoughts and words. *Paśyantī*, the spiritual flash transferred into the upper, deeper reaches of mind as "seen" by a seer wordlessly. *Madhyamā* is when it comes to the mental verbal speech, and finally *vaikharī*, the variety of speech *brayed* as syllabic sound by the human "donkey". This is the process of revelation whereby the seer receives internal knowledge and translates it into words for the human listeners. Here, *sa-nāmā* does not resort to the last level as he passes on the knowledge in a direct mind to mind transfer.

[25] *Mānasa-putra* or *mānasa-śiṣya*. The closest disciples may be referred to thus as their mind is born of the seminal seed of the *guru*'s mind.

Here are 109 of the approximately 3,000 names that we received:[26]

śrīṁ a'īṁ hrīṁ klīṁ krīṁ śrīṁ | [27]

1. Who is the meaning of the word "That", who is the meaning of the word "thou", meaning of the word "art";[28]
2. Centre of the axle of great spheres of a myriad polar stars;
3. Who wears the *suṣumṇā-svara*[29] as her garment;
4. Who is the brilliant one sitting on the lotus seat in the Mind lake;
5. Who is the flame of the divine Names;
6. Who is the Lady of the uncountable million moons;
7. Who is the sister, daughter, wife, beautiful bride;
8. Who wears the hair ornament upholding the brilliance of jewels that are a million trillion universes concealed

[26] There are approximately 3,000 names that flashed into this disciple's mind and were recorded on paper as they appeared. They cannot all be translated here. In the Sanskrit composition there are many incidents of *chando-bhaṅga,* metrical irregularities which we have not attempted to correct as we did not wish to interfere with the way they appeared.

[27] It is a normal Indian tradition to begin a text with divine remembrance. Here some of the key *bīja-mantra*s (seed words) are recited before starting the text.

[28] "That thou art", *tat tvam asi,* one of the key "mega sentences" in Vedānta used for deep contemplation till its meaning dawns in the consciousness.

[29] When both nostrils flow with equal force evenly and the consciousness enters the central stream of *kuṇḍalinī.*

in the coiffure of her hair;

9. Who is the power of dissolving the waves of recitation of *mantras* into silence;
10. Who wears the crown of purest crystal;
11. Who confers containment of the energy of excitation in the agitated;
12. Who wanders inside the *maṇḍalas*;
13. Who is occupied in bursting through the knots;
14. Whose rays are the sun and the moon that traverse the nostrils;
15. Who enjoys the ecstasy of spaces;
16 Who makes spaces dance;
17. Who nurses on her breast the infants that are the immeasurable universes (*brahmāṇḍa*);
18. Who belongs to and is playful in infants;
19. Who is to be found through infancy;
20. Who turns to ashes the five elements;
21. Who is the ground of all ashes;
22. Who is equally the meaning of the verbs "to be" and "to do";
23. Who is the desire for being;
24. Who casts the lightless shadow called concept of "I am body";
25. Who banishes the shadow of the concept of "I am body";
26. Who awakens the wisdom "I am not body";
27. Whose body is chrism composed of the aloe-wood essence, sandalwood fragrance and camphor of the five elements;

28. Who wanders inside the intersticial spaces of minute atoms and universes alike;
29. Who is the ascetic endeavour (*sādhanā*) of the *mantra*s that please the deity called All-Women;
30. Who eats duality as food;
31. Who abolishes secret sins;
32. Who is worshipped by a billion frolicking beautiful celestial nymphs who bear the bodies made of light of the pathways of energy-channels coursing through the great groves that flourish inside the jewel of the minutest point (*bindu*);
33. Who has absorbed all the great flames into herself;
34. Who miraculously vibrates in the form of the pleasure that is experienced in the senses;
35. Who has a thousand eyes, a thousand rays, a thousand feet, and thousands of teeth for eating uncountable trillion universes;
36. Who is the digestive power;
37. Who dances the dance of consumption in the form of the uncountable flames that dance inside the womb of uncountable suns;
38. Who is the sharp razor blade endowed with the knowledge to cut through the hard rocks of our afflictions;
39. Who destroys the divisions among all nations;
40. Who abolishes yesterdays and tomorrows into a single flow of time;
41. Who is the love in the billion, trillion kisses and hugs that are going on in this entire universe at this very time;

42. Who is the *vīṇā*, stringed instrument, with a thousand strings;
43. Who maintains femininity in the male body;
44. Who maintains masculinity in the female body;
45. Who merges the male and the female;
46. Who is the lady that rules the life force of the vowel that supports the consonant;
47. Who is the dancing flame of names;
48. Who institutes the cycles of seasons;
49. Who takes a ride on the wheels of seasons;
50. Who wears the seasonal flowers as her robes;
51. Who wakes all beings to those seasons;
52. Who lives in the reservoirs called morning and evening;
53. Who rules over all *mantra*s;
54. Who is the fire inside the womb of the Earth;
55. Who is the burning lava flow emanating from the ground;[30]
56. Who is the luminosity inside the jewel;
57. Who is the gleam of the silver and the gold;
58. Who has made her home inside the wombs of countless suns;
59. Who is the pollinating[31] woman;

---

[30] The tāntric meaning of this would be the energy spilled out from *mūlādhāra cakra*. This is given here only as an example of the hidden meaning of these phrases.

[31] The most common Sanskrit word for a menstruating woman is *rajasvalā*, pollinating one.

60. Who is flowering;[32]
61. Who is the awakening of the vibration in *japa*;
62. Who turns the words into a vibration;
63. Who excites all;
64. Who pacifies all excitations;
65. Who is earned in the coins of breath;
66. Whose body is breath;
67. Whose worship is in breath;
68. Who loves breaths;
69. Who has breath as her lover;
70. Who is the mouth of the whole universe to consume;
71. Who is Mother of heavens having moons for riding chariots;
72. Who wanders secretly inside the curves of the conch-shells of galaxies;
73. Who wanders in secret inside the curves of the conch-shells of a thousand million universes;
74. Who wears space as her shawl;
75. Whose lion throne is a point (*bindu*);
76. Who measures the depth of 100 oceans;
77. Who is ours;
78. Who is yours;
79. Who is all this;
80. Who is the creator of mind fields;

---

[32] Other Sanskrit words for a menstruating woman mean: blossoming one, flowering one.

81. Who is the nourisher and sustainer of mind fields;
82. Who is the dissolver of mind fields;
83. One from whom the moon receives its smile;
84. Who eats and digests spaces;
85. Who is intent upon withdrawal of the sensations of all the senses;
86. Whose anklet bells are always chiming as she incessantly dances in the cave theatre of *anāhata*, the heart centre;
87. Who is Allah, Yahweh, Maria;
88. Who has incarnated in the body of Yeshu;
89. Who wears the flower-like beautiful minds for her *mālā*;[33]
90. The in-dweller, the out-dweller, reaching to the closest, reaching to the farthest;
91. Having long hairs called spaces;
92. Who is ruling deity of all sacred places of pilgrimage;
93. Who merges the meanings of one, two, three and many so that they may not be known separately;
94. Ever delicious, ever to be tasted;
95. Who is the sharp razor edge to cut the hard rocks of the darkness of ignorance;
96. Sweet honey-wine of gods;
97. Who is the music and her own musical instrument;
98. Who roams freely in the vast hallways inside the interior point (*bindu*) wherein the supporting pillars are the uncountable galaxies and universes;

---

[33] The rosary of the *yogīs*.

99. Who dances solo in the theatre hall inside the point (*bindu*) of the immeasurable vast *maṇḍala* drawn of flames of the universes;
100. Great goddess of resonance, consonance and conviviance;[34]
101. Whose musical rhythm is kept in the melodies of light;
102. Who is the letter "ee" and letter "l";[35]
103. Who is error and who is reality;
104. Ladle of fullness to be heated by lightning;
105. Who sits in the centre of the *maṇḍala* of cave-dwelling *yogīs*;
106. Who consumes petals of lotuses;
107. Breaker of the chains of those bound;
108. Whose smile is the manifestation and dissolution of universes;
109. Whose name is heard in all names.

Having thus received experiential knowledge by the power of these names from the *guru*'s consciousness in a billionth part of an in-wink,[36] He then came into out-wink again.

---

[34] English adaptation for Spanish convivencia or Italian convivnza, meaning living together, sharing life-force together.

[35] These are secrets in the *mantra* science.

[36] In-wink (*nimeṣa*) and out-wink (*unmeṣa*) are a measure to express shortest possible time in many Indo-European languages, for example, German Augenblick. In the philosophy of consciousness, as in Kāśmīr Śaivism, it has a much deeper significance. The creation of the universe is God out-winking, and dissolution of the universe is God in-blinking. An entire cycle of creation and dissolution →

This out-wink, of the nature of spaces, times, names and forms, overtook him as he prepared to pass on the knowledge to his own disciples.

But he himself stayed in the secret cavern.[37]

Joyfully did he stay in the *guru*'s earthly *āśrama* through his physical life as he banished the confusions of those who remain lost in the mazes of spaces, times and solids and senses, leading them through purifications.

He awakened the common people who are deluded, with their experiential knowledge lying asleep; he repeatedly awakens them from the fog of confusion for the sake of their enlightenment.

He, himself now the *guru*, showed to these disciples the path of the highest pleasure that is the way of supreme liberation.

As to those of his disciples who are qualified and capacious — he makes them enter this middle way of *suṣumṇā*. Their she-snake, the *kuṇḍalinī*, he awakens

- by a glance of his eye,
- by the *mantra* voice, or
- by the vibration in his hand.[38]

→ of the universes occurs in one eye-blink of God. Also, when one enters deepest consciousness to receive knowledge, that is in-blink and when one emerges from that it is out-blink of a practitioner of *samādhi*.

[37] One must remain in the interior cavern of attunement with divine consciousness to pass on the knowledge to disciples even when one appears to be speaking words. That is the well-kept secret of teaching meditation.

[38] The three methods of *yoga* initiations. The fourth one, much higher, is indicated in the following verse.

Or, meditating upon his *guru*, radiating his consciousness into theirs, he, one with the self of *yoga*, initiates them, thus uniting them with the *guru*'s consciousness.

He causes them to enter all internal caves of the drop of light, drop of sound;[39] establishes them right there on the seat of consciousness.

While he, the compassionate one, is engaged upon liberating many people, all the while he remains attuned to the consciousness-alone *guru* in his own self.

He spins and weaves the fabric of *samādhi*, not permitting the thread to break at all. Sitting in the grotto of consciousness he grants to many such a grace.

Thus simultaneous resident of both worlds, granted ever new life by *kuṇḍalinī*, he lived a thousand human years and then went into the status of *kaivalya*, the Consciousness-solo.

Thus whosoever, wading unceasingly in the middle of the consciousness-stream, would let oneself meditate upon even a single name of *kuṇḍalinī* on the path of *suṣumṇā*, or simply remember even one name of *kuṇḍalinī* forming a *mantra* by prefixing *śrīṁ*, converting the name to dative case and ending with the word *namaḥ*,[40] and, being wise, let him lead the *mantra* to ascend and descend through *prāṇa* and through the lotus-ponds of *cakra*s,

- swimming through them,

---

[39] Titles of two of the Upaniṣads, *tejo-bindu* and *nāda-bindu*, referring to the concealed point of consciousness the "fissioning" of which is referred to elsewhere in this presentation.

[40] For example, if we take the name *kuṇḍalinī*, the *mantra* will be formed as *śrīṁ kuṇḍalinyai namaḥ*.

- with even breath —

thus should one traverse the *meru* channel.[41]

Having fully renounced the *siddhis*,[42] firm on the vow of *samādhi*, such a one will live healthy and free of illnesses as long as he wishes.

Fissioning the central point of vibration, entering into its gate when dropping the body with a smile, he would enter *nirvāṇa*; abandoning the weight of this physical body he would be in a free flight and then he would make his dwelling in a cottage made of his own light in some.

Nowhere-Void, unencumbered by the delimitations of space, time and such, with his light freed into independence he will fly in the bliss of the ultimate perfect enlightenment (*samyag-bodhi*); he may even go beyond the status of *kaivalya*.

---

[41] *Meru*, one of the core words in Indian spiritual tradition; the central mountain of the universe (not merely of planet earth), the spine. Here, the channel of energy is passing through the spine.

[42] So-known "supernatural" powers. It is required of the true aspirant seeking spiritual liberation to renounce these just as one renounces the worldly powers.

Bibliography

Arya, Pandit Usharbudh (Swami Veda Bharati), *Mantra & Meditation: Superconscious Meditation*, vol. II, Honesdale, PA: The Himalayan International Institute of Yoga Science and Philosophy, 1981.

"Energy of Consciousness in Human Personality" in Ronald S. Valle and Rolf von Eckartsberg (eds.), *Metaphors of Consciousness*, New York and London: Plenum Press, 1981, 1989.

Silburn, Lillian (tr.), *Kundalini: Energy of the Depths*, Albany, NY: State University of New York (SUNY) Press, 1988.

Swami Rama, *Sacred Journey: Living Purposefully and Dying Gracefully*, Dehradun: The Himalayan International Hospital Trust, distributed by Lotus Press, Twin Lakes, WI, 2002.

———, *Subtler than the Subtle: The Upanishad of the White Horse*, Saint Paul, MN: Yes International Publishers, 2002.

———, *Wisdom of the Ancient Sages: Mundaka Upanishad*, Honesdale, PA: The Himalayan International Institute of Yoga Science and Philosophy, 1990, pp. 28, 56, 60, 163.

———, *Path of Fire and Light*, vol. II: *A Practical Companion to Volume I*, Honesdale, PA: The Himalayan International Institute of Yoga Science and Philosophy, 1988, pp. 83, 91, 151-78, 211.

———, *Path of Fire and Light*, vol. I: *Advanced Practices in Yoga*, Honesdale, PA: The Himalayan International Institute of Yoga Science and Philosophy, 1986, pp. 7, 9, 33, 42, 50-51, 54, 60-61, 76, 92, 110, 122, 129-39, 143-60.

———, *Perennial Psychology of the Bhagavad Gita*, Honesdale, PA: The Himalayan International Institute of Yoga Science and Philosophy, 1985, p. 339.

———, *Inspired Thoughts,* Honesdale, PA: The Himalayan International Institute of Yoga Science and Philosophy, 1983, pp. 211-30.

———, *Life Here and Hereafter,* Honesdale, PA: The Himalayan International Institute of Yoga Science and Philosophy, 1976.

Swami Rama, Rudolph Ballentine and Alan Hymes, *Science of Breath: A Practical Guide,* Honesdale, PA: The Himalayan International Institute of Yoga Science and Philosophy, 1979.

Swami Rama, Rudolph Ballentine and Swami Ajaya, *Yoga and Psychotherapy: The Evolution of Consciousness,* Honesdale, PA: Himalayan Publishers, 1976.

White, John (ed.), *Kundalini: Evolution and Enlightenment,* New York: Paragon House, 1990.

Woodroffe, Sir John and Sir John Arthur Avalon, *The Serpent Power,* repr., Chennai: Ganesha & Co., 2003.

Audio tapes recommended for the Kuṇḍalinī Study
by Swami Veda Bharati

1. The Cakras: An Intensive Study (5)
2. Kuṇḍalinī and the Seven Centres of Consciousness (10)
3. Śrī Vidyā (12)
4. Śrī (2)
5. Kuṇḍalinī (two lectures given in Budapest, 2012).

Ask availability of the recordings to:
<ahymsinpublishers@gmail.com>

Index

Our Lineage (Guru-Paramparā)

In Gurudeva Swami Rama a number of lineages merge.

Through his Yoga-Guru Bangali Maharaj he represents the tradition of the Himalayan *yogī*s.

In Vedānta, the tradition goes all the way to the ancient history of Vedānta, through Śaṅkarācārya and Vidyāraṇya Muni, with the seat at Śṛṅgerī.

In *saṁnyāsa*, it goes all the way to the Vedic times and then through Śaṅkarācārya's Daśanāmī order, with Bhāratī lineage, with the seat at Śṛṅgerī.

In Christianity, it goes all the way to Christ's chief disciple St. Peter. How is that? The mystery of that is known to few close disciples.

In the Buddhist tradition, as he had told me at the time of my *yoga*-initiation, we are preparing the grounds for the coming of Maitreya Buddha.

We inherit the Tibetan tradition through the Tibetan master who was the *guru* of the Gurudeva of Swami Rama.

We inherit the *bhakti* tradition through Madhusūdana Sarasvatī, a former birth of Swami Rama (who introduced *bhakti* into Vedānta) in sixteenth century.

Swami Veda was practically born expounding Vedas and the Sūtras of Patañjali, a fact attributed by the learned of that time to the knowledge from his previous births. So we inherit the Vedic and Patañjali tradition in this form also.

This convergence of diverse traditions is one of our greatest spiritual strengths.

Swami Veda Bharati

Chancellor, HIHT University, Dehra Dun

BORN in a Sanskrit-speaking family in 1933, Swami Veda Bharati started teaching the *Yoga-Sūtras* of Patañjali from 1942, at the age of nine.

In 1946 a number of articles appeared in the Hindi press proclaiming this child prodigy's exceptional knowledge of the Vedas. He then began to be invited to address crowds of thousands as well as colleges and universities throughout north India.

From February 1947 he has been travelling worldwide giving discourses and establishing meditation centres. He has, to his credit, 4,000 hours of recorded lectures on history, philosophy and practices of meditation and has written eighteen books including a 1,500-page commentary on the first two *pada*s of the *Yoga-Sūtras,* a highly scholarly and meticulous work.

Between 1965 and 1967 he obtained all his degrees: BA (Honours) London, MA (London), D.Litt. (Holland), and FRAS. He has varying degrees of depth in seventeen languages.

In 1969 he met his *yoga guru* Swami Rama of Himalayas (author of *Living with Himalayan Masters*) who initiated him into the highest path of *dhyāna-yoga*.

Swami Veda Bharati teaches meditation from within the religious, spiritual and literary traditions of different world cultures — from China to Africa — to different parts of Europe. In each culture he teaches meditation from within that culture, for example, in Italy he teaches Dante's *Il Paradiso* as a text of the experience of divine light in meditation; he is visited by masters of the Sūfī orders; and has forty-five hours of recordings of lectures on Christian traditions of meditation.

He has also been engaged in neurological research in meditation and maintains a sophisticated laboratory in his *āśrama* for testing brain waves and other neuro-physiological patterns during meditation.

He runs over fifty meditation groups and centres in twenty-five countries; holds the prestigious title of Mahāmaṇḍaleśvara in the community of the Swami Order of monks; is spiritual guide to two *āśrama*s in Rishikesh where seekers from twenty-five countries come to learn meditation and undergo varying periods of guided silence.

Swami Veda Bharati also maintains keen interest in the relationship of science and meditation, runs a research laboratory at his *Āśrama* measuring the psycho-neuro-physiological responses to the different practices of meditation.

In that context, he has been the subject of several experiments in the neurology of meditation in institutions like the Institute of Noetic Sciences, California; in a unique experiment, sitting outside a Faraday Chamber, he blocked the photon beams in an interferometer, which was inside the chamber, nine times in a row, proving the power of the volition of consciousness over material energies. The results of this experiment have been published in the Scientific Press.

He also spends much of his time travelling worldwide, lecturing and participating in relevant conferences and giving guidance to sixty meditation groups on all continents.

The author plans to enter a five- or seven-year period of silence from March 2013.

Among his academic publications see:

1. "Consciousness: Measurable or Immeasurable?", papers read at an International Seminar held at the Ramakrishna Mission Institute of Culture, Kolkata, 2010, published in *Spirituality and Science of Consciousness*, Kolkata: Ramakrishna Mission Institute

of Culture, 2011, pp. 116-41 and 411-14.

2. "Shanti: An Indian Perspective" in Wolfgang Dietrich et al. (eds.) *The Palgrave International Handbook of Peace Studies: A Cultural Perspective*, London and New York: Unesco Chair of Peace Studies (University of Innsbruck, Austria) and Palgrave Macmillan, 2011, pp. 191-228.

www.swamiveda.org, www.swmivedablog.org

Other Books by the Author

- *Night Birds*
- *Education and Parenting for Peace*
- *Light of Ten Thousand Suns* (Poems)
- *Mantra: The Sacred Chants*
- *Meditation: The Art and Science*
- *Meditation and the Art of Dying*
- *Philosophy of Hatha Yoga*
- *108 Blossoms from Guru Grant Garden*
- *Shanti: Inner Meaning and Experience*
- *Yogi in the Lab*
- *Yoga-Sutras of Patanjali* (vols. I & II)
- and many more books, audios and CDs.

For full catalogue of books and CDs/DVDs, contact:

AHYMSIN Publishers

Swami Rama Sadhaka Grama (SRSG)

Virpur Khurd, Virbhadra Road

Rishikesh – 249 203 (India)

Tel: +91-135-2453030

e-mail: ahymsinpublishers@gmail.com,

info@ahymsin.in

www.ahymsin.in